OUT & ABOUT

• WALKING GUIDES TO BRITAIN •

No 6

Southern England

MARSHALL CAVENDISH

First published in Great Britain in 1995 by
Marshall Cavendish Books, London
(a division of Marshall Cavendish Partworks Ltd)

Copyright © 1995 Marshall Cavendish

All maps in this publication are reproduced from Ordnance Survey 1:25,000 maps with the permission of
The Controller of Her Majesty's Stationery Office, © Crown copyright.

ISBN 03190 057 8X

British Library Cataloguing in Publication Data:
A catalogue record for this book is available from the British Library

Printed and bound in Dubai, U.A.E.

Some of this material has previously appeared in the Marshall Cavendish partwork *OUT & ABOUT*

CONTENTS

Introduction to

OUT & ABOUT

• WALKING GUIDES TO BRITAIN •

Walking has become one of the most popular pastimes in Britain. To enjoy walking, you don't need any special skills, you don't have to follow rules or join expensive clubs, and you don't need any special equipment – though a pair of walking boots is a good idea! It is an easy way of relaxing and getting some exercise, and of enjoying nature and the changing seasons.

The OUT & ABOUT WALKING GUIDES TO BRITAIN will give you ideas for walks in your own neighbourhood and in other areas of Britain. All the walks are devised around a theme and range in length from about 2 to 9 miles (3.25 to 14.5 km) and in difficulty from very easy to mildly strenuous. Since each walk is circular, you will always be able to get back to your starting point.

Devised by experts and tested for accuracy, all the walks are accompanied by clear, practical instructions and an enlarged section of the relevant Ordnance Survey map. The flavour of the walk and highlights to look out for are described in the introductory text.

LOCAL COLOUR

Background features give you extra insight into item of local interest. The OUT & ABOUT WALKING GUIDES TO BRITAIN relate legends, point out unusual architectural details, provide a potted his tory of the lives of famous writers and artists connected with a particular place, explain traditional crafts still practised by local artisans, and uncover the secrets behind an ever-changing landscape.

DISCOVER NATURE

One of the greatest pleasures in going for a walk i the sense of being close to nature. On the walks suggested in the OUT & ABOUT WALKING GUIDES TO BRITAIN, you can feel the wind, smell the pine trees, hear the birds and see the beauty of the countryside. You will become more aware of the seasons – the life cycles of butterflies the mating calls of birds, the protective behaviour of all creatures with their young. You will see the beginning of new life in the forests and fields, the bluebell carpets in spring woodlands, the dazzling beauty of rhododendron bushes in early summer, the swaying cornfields of summer and the golden colours of leaves in autumn. The OUT & ABOUT WALKING GUIDES TO BRITAIN tell you what to look out for and where to find it.

NATURE WALK

Occasional nature walk panels. will highlight an interesting feature that you will see on your walk. You will learn about natural and manmade details in the landscape, how to tell which animal or bird has nibbled the cones in a pine forest, what nurse trees are and what a triangulation point is.

FACT FILE

The fact file will give you at-a-glance information about each walk to help you make your selection.

✳	**general location**
os	**map reference for Ordnance Survey map with grid reference for starting point**
	length of the walk in miles and kilometres
	time needed if walking at an average speed
	character of the walk: easy/easy with strenuous parts/mildly strenuous; hills to be climbed and muddy or dangerous areas are pointed out
P	**parking facilities near the start of the walk**
T	**public transport information**
	facilities for refreshment, including pubs serving lunchtime meals, restaurants, tea rooms and picnic areas
WC	**location of toilets**
	historic sites

```
miles 0   1   2   3   4   5   6   7   8   9
kms   0 1 2 3 4 5 6 7 8 9 10 11 12 13 14 15
```

ORDNANCE SURVEY MAPS

All the walks in the OUT & ABOUT WALKING GUIDES TO BRITAIN are illustrated on large-scale, full-colour maps supplied by the Ordnance Survey. Ordnance Survey are justifiably proud of their worldwide reputation for excellence and accuracy. For extra clarity, the maps have been enlarged to a scale of 1:21,120 (3 inches to 1 mile).

The route for each walk is marked clearly on the map with a broken red line, and the numbers along the

ABOVE: *Colourful narrowboats are always an attractive feature on inland waterways.*

route refer you to the numbered stages in the written directions. In addition, points of interest are marked on the maps with letters. Each one is mentioned in the walk directions and is described in detail in the introductory text.

COUNTRYWISE

The countryside is one of our greatest resources. If we treat it with respect, we can preserve it for the future.

Throughout the countryside there is a network of paths and byways. Some are former trading routes, others are simply the paths villagers took to visit one another in the days before public transport. Most are designated 'rights of way': foot-paths, open only to people on foot, and bridleways, open to people on foot, horseback or bicycle. These paths can be identified on Ordnance Survey maps and verified, in cases of dispute, by the definitive map for the area, held by the relevant local authority.

THE LAW OF TRESPASS

If you find a public right of way barred to you, you may remove the obstruction or take a short detour around it. However, in England and Wales, if you stray from the footpath you are trespassing and could be sued in a civil court for damages. In Scotland, rights of way are not recorded on definitive maps, nor is there a law of trespass. Although you may cross mountain and moorland paths, landowners are permitted to impose restrictions on access, such as during the grouse-shooting season, which should be obeyed.

If you are following a public right of way and find, for example, that your path is blocked by a field of crops, you are entitled to walk the line of the footpath through the crops, in single file. Farmers are required, by law, to restore public rights of way within 14 days of ploughing. However, if you feel uncomfortable about doing this and can find a way round, then do so. But report the matter to the local authority who will take the necessary action to clear the correct route.

RIGHT: *The stunning patchwork of fields surrounding the picturesque village of Widecombe in the heart of Dartmoor makes a beautiful setting for the famous annual fair.*
BELOW: *Brown hares boxing in spring are a fascinating sight.*

It is illegal for farmers to place a bull on its own in a field crossed by a right of way (unless the bull is not a recognized dairy breed). If you come across a bull alone in a field, find another way round.

COMMONS AND PARKS

There are certain areas in England and Wales where you may be able to wander without keeping to paths, such as most commons and beaches. There are also country parks, set up by local authorities for public recreation – parkland, woodland, heath or farmland.

The National Trust is the largest private landowner in England and Wales. Its purpose is to preserve areas of natural beauty and sites of historic interest by acquisition, holding them in trust for public access and enjoyment. Information on access may be obtained from National Trust headquarters at

THE COUNTRY CODE

- **Enjoy the countryside, and respect its life and work**

- **Always guard against risk of fire**

- **Fasten all gates**

- **Keep your dogs under close control**

- **Keep to public footpaths across farmland**

- **Use gates and stiles to cross fences, hedges and walls**

- **Leave livestock, crops and machinery alone**

- **Take your litter home**

- **Help to keep all water clean**

- **Protect wildlife, plants and trees**

- **Take special care on country roads**

- **Make no unnecessary noise**

6 QueenAnne's Gate, London SW1H 9AS
Tel: 071-222 9251.

Most regions of great scenic beauty in England and Wales are designated National Parks or Areas of Outstanding Natural Beauty (AONB). In Scotland, they are known as National Scenic Areas (NSAs) or AONBs.

Most of this land is privately owned and there is no right of public access. In some cases, local authorities may have negotiated agreements with landowners to allow walkers access on mountains and moors.

CONSERVATION
National park, AONB or NSA status is intended to provide some measure of protection for the landscape, guarding against unsuitable development while encouraging enjoyment of its natural beauty.

ABOVE RIGHT *Carelessness with cigarettes, matches or camp fires can be devastating in a forest.*

Nature reserves are areas set aside for conservation. Most are privately owned, some by large organizations such as the Royal Society for the Protection of Birds. Although some offer public access, most require permission to enter.

THE RAMBLERS ASSOCIATION
The aims of the Ramblers Association are to further greater understanding and care of the countryside, to protect and enhance public rights of way and areas of natural beauty, to improve public access to the countryside, and to encourage more people to take up rambling as a healthy, recreational activity. It has played an important role in preserving and developing our national footpath network.

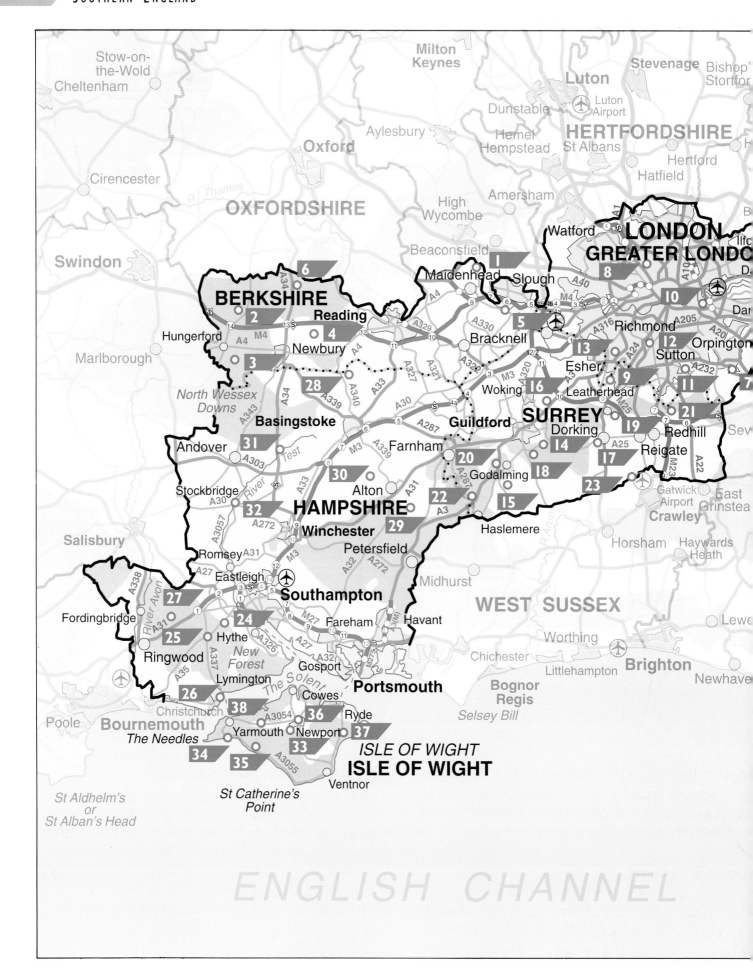

Southern England

All the walks featured in this book are plotted and numbered on the regional map (left) and listed in the box below.

USING MAPS

Although the OUT & ABOUT WALKING GUIDES TO BRITAIN give you all the information you need, it is useful to have some basic map skills. Most of us have some experience of using a motoring atlas to navigate by car. Navigating when walking is much the same, except that mistakes are much more time and energy consuming and, if circumstances conspire, could lead to an accident.

A large-scale map is the answer to identifying where you are. Britain is fortunate in having the best mapping agency in the world, the Ordnance Survey, which produces high-quality maps, the most popular being the 1:50,000 Landranger series. However, the most useful for walkers are the 1:25,000 Pathfinder, Explorer and Outdoor Leisure maps.

THE LIE OF THE LAND

A map provides more than just a bird's eye view of the land; it also conveys information about the terrain – whether marshy, forested, covered with tussocky grass or boulders; it distinguishes between footpaths and bridleways; and shows boundaries such as parish and county boundaries.

Symbols are used to identify a variety of landmarks such as churches, camp and caravan sites, bus, coach and rail stations, castles, caves and historic houses. Perhaps most importantly of all, the shape of the land is indicated by contour lines. Each line represents land at a specific height so it is possible to read the gradient from the spacing of the lines (the closer the spacing, the steeper the hill).

GRID REFERENCES

All Ordnance Survey maps are over-printed with a framework of squares known as the National Grid. This is a reference system which, by breaking the country down into squares, allows you to pinpoint any place in the country and give it a unique reference number; very useful when making rendezvous arrangements. On OS Landranger, Pathfinder and Outdoor Leisure maps it is possible to give a reference to an accuarcy of 100 metres. Grid squares on these maps cover an area of 1 km x 1 km on the ground.

GIVING A GRID REFERENCE

Blenheim Palace in Oxfordshire has a grid reference of **SP 441 161**. This is constructed as follows:

SP These letters identify the 100 km grid square in which Blenheim Palace lies. These squares form the basis of the National Grid. Information on the

100 km square covering a particular map is always given in the map key.

441 161 This six figure reference locates the position of Blenheim Palace to 100 metres in the 100 km grid square.

44 This part of the reference is the number of the grid line which forms the western (left-hand) boundary of the 1 km grid square in which Blenheim Palace appears. This number is printed in the top and bottom margins of the relevant OS map (Pathfinder 1092 in this case).

16 This part of the reference is the number of the grid line which forms the southern (lower) boundary of the 1 km grid square in which Blenheim Palace appears. This number is printed in the left- and right-hand margins of the relevant OS map (Pathfinder 1092).

These two numbers together (SP 4416) locate the bottom left-hand corner of

the 1 km grid square in which Blenheim Palace appears. The remaining figures in the reference **441 161** pinpoint the position within that square by dividing its western boundary lines into tenths and estimating on which imaginary tenths line Blenheim Palace lies.

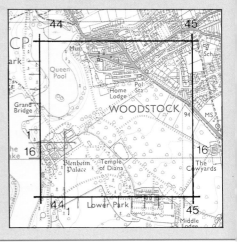

AN ARTIST'S INSPIRATION

BERKSHIRE

A Thameside walk through a village of 'heavenly visitations'

DEREK FORSS. INSET: JEFF GOODMAN/NHPA

The Thameside village of Cookham has been made famous by its use as a setting for many of the paintings of Sir Stanley Spencer. The artist was born in a house in the High Street some 100 years ago. There is now a permanent exhibition of his work in the Stanley Spencer Gallery ● in the former Victorian Methodist chapel that he attended as a child. To Spencer, Cookham was the scene of 'heavenly visitations', and the river with its boat yards, the village and the parish church all form a backdrop to his religious paintings.

FACT FILE

* ☀ Cookham-on-Thames, Berkshire on A4094, 4 miles (7 km) south of M40, junction 3

* ▭ Explorer 3, grid reference 892353

miles 0 1 2 3 4 5 6 7 8 9 10 miles
kms 0 1 2 3 4 5 6 7 8 9 10 11 12 13 14 15 kms

* ◷ Allow 2¹/2 hours

* ▬ Easy walking over level ground

* P National Trust Car Park (free); Cookham Moor 219 yards (200 metres) west of Cookham High Street

* T Access to transportation from BR Station in Cookham, ¹/2 mile (800 metres)

* ⍭ Refreshments in Cookham

* ⌂ Stanley Spencer Gallery open Easter-October daily (inc. weekends) 10.30 am-5.30 pm; November-Easter Saturday, Sunday and Bank Holidays 11.00 am-5.00 pm. Cliveden: National Trust grounds open March-December daily; House open April-October, Thursday and Sunday pm

The walk not only encompasses the lovely little village, with its half-timbered houses, but includes one of the most beautiful stretches of the Thames at Cliveden Reach. High above, on the opposite bank, is Cliveden itself, the great house ● built for the Duke of Sutherland.

THE IRON BRIDGE

The route starts at Cookham Moor, the ancient common land adjacent to the village. A short walk across fields brings you to the towpath of the River Thames.

Walking towards the iron bridge of Cookham, where once a toll was charged, the octagonal toll house ●

▲ *The Thames at Cookham is tranquil in winter; in summer pleasure boats share the river with anglers catching such fish as perch (inset).*

is visible on the opposite bank. Just short of the bridge, a path leads up through Cookham churchyard ●, the setting for *The Resurrection*, the most controversial of Spencer's paintings. On reaching the High Street you encounter the 'Bel and Dragon'. The most interesting of the many old buildings, it was estab-

▼ **Cookham from Cookham Dean** *was painted by Spencer (1891-1959), nicknamed Cookham at the Slade.*

BRADFORD ART GALLERY/BRIDGEMAN, LONDON

COOKHAM – WIDBROOK COMMON

The walk begins at the National Trust car park at Cookham Moor, 219 yards (200 metres) west of Cookham High Street.

1 From the car park follow the footpath across the green, signposted to Cockmarsh, to a step-stile in the hedge into a field. Follow the clear path across the field to the towpath beside the river. Turn right along the towpath and follow the permitted path in front of the Cookham Reach Sailing Club.

2 With Cookham bridge 100 yards (90 metres) or so ahead and the octagonal toll house **A** visible on the opposite bank, turn right along a path and enter Cookham churchyard **B** through a swing-gate. Continue through the churchyard and enter a small square called Churchgate. Here, turn left and after a few paces turn right along the pavement. Cross the High Street to the Stanley Spencer Gallery **C** and continue ahead along Sutton Road for 100 yards (91.5 metres) to a small crossroads.

3 Turn left down Mill Lane and follow this lane for about ¹/2 mile (800 metres) to a private road sign. Turn right here along a footpath that runs through trees, parallel to a metalled drive. When this drive reaches a small bridge, follow the footpath sharply right, with a field on your right, through the trees to the River Thames. Opposite are Cliveden House grounds **D**.

4 Turn right along the towpath and, with the river on your left, follow this path along the bank for 1 mile (1.6 km), passing islands **E** in midstream. Shortly after passing the islands, the towpath passes the edge of a wood and a line of larch trees. Just after crossing a small bridge in front of Islet Park House, turn right along a lane leading to Islet Road. Follow this road for 250 yards (229 metres) to a crossroads. Cross to the pavement on the opposite side and turn right along the road, passing Hitachi Park **F** on your right.

5 Continue for ¹/4 mile (400 metres) to a 'Road Narrows' sign. Here, turn left through a wooden swing-gate on to Widbrook Common. Follow the path across the common, with the White Brook now on your right, to a bridge. Cross

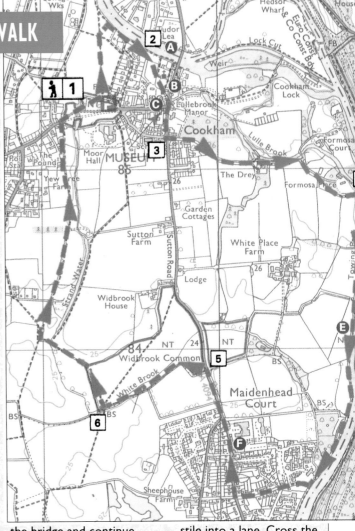

the bridge and continue ahead, with a hedge on your left, to a stile. Cross the stile and continue along the path over a small bridge that crosses a little stream.

6 Just before reaching a second bridge, turn right over a stile into a field. Cross the field, walking slightly right, to another

stile into a lane. Cross the lane to a stile opposite and follow the path between wire fences. After a short distance, the path crosses another stile and continues ahead along the edge of a field beside a hedge. Follow this path for ¹/2 mile (800 metres) to a road. Turn right, over a red brick bridge to arrive back at the car park.

---

lished in the reign of Henry V and claims the distinction of being one of the oldest inns in England. Almost opposite is the Spencer Gallery.

Mill Lane takes you out of the village, through fields and to a woodland path. This path withholds its surprise to the last moment: suddenly you arrive on the river bank. The setting is quite magnificent for across the river, the extensive and lovely grounds of Cliveden sweep down to the water's edge.

After following the towpath for the best part of 1 mile (1.6 km) you reach some islands in midstream **E**. After leaving the river you pass the modern pavilions of the Hitachi Park building **F**. How different, only moments later, to arrive at the National Trust's Widbrook Common. From here a pleasant field path returns you to Cookham Moor and the car park.

▶ *Cookham churchyard, where Spencer's body lies, features in many of his visionary paintings.*

DEREK FORSS

HORSES AND COURSES

ROB SCOTT. INSET: GDT-SILVESTRIS/NHPA

A walk on open downland and along a disused railway

Lambourn Valley is racehorse country. There are racing stables down in the valley and gallops where the horses are exercised and trained on the hills above.

The walk begins in the charming village of East Garston **A**. It is spread out along the River Lambourn, which in dry weather is no more than a trickle and sometimes even disappears altogether. The older village houses reflect the fact that good building stone is virtually nonexistent in this area. Almost all the cottages are timber-framed, but a rich variety of materials has been used to fill in the walls. Brick is a common material. Sometimes light-coloured 'headers' — bricks laid at right angles to the face of the wall so that only their

FACT FILE

* East Garston, 3 miles (5 km) south-east of Lambourn

* Pathfinders 1154 (SU 28/38) and 1170 (SU 27/37), grid reference SU 362768

miles 0 1 2 3 4 5 6 7 8 9 10 miles
kms 0 1 2 3 4 5 6 7 8 9 10 11 12 13 14 15 kms

* Allow 3 hours

* Steep in places and some paths are muddy when wet

* **P** East Garston village

* Public house and shop at East Garston and Eastbury

'heads' show — alternate with darker 'stretchers' to create a chequered effect, known as diaper work. Interesting effects are also created by using knobbly flints for walls and there is a particularly attractive use of tiles on a gable end at Church

▲ *The Lambourn Valley has a racing tradition, but in East Garston some people ride just for the pleasure of it. On the surrounding downs, hares (inset) can be found 'boxing' in spring.*

Cottage, near the beginning of the walk. Thatch is widely used for roofing, sometimes sweeping in attractive curves round tiny first-floor windows: there is even a house that boasts a thatched garage. One very attractive feature is the use of little footbridges across the river to link cottages on the south bank.

FARMYARD

The road swings round towards the church and ends in a broad track that runs through the farmyard of Manor Farm. On the right is a group of stables, but although these are the first to be met along the walk, it is unlikely that you will have come this far without at least a glimpse of a horse. The village street regularly echoes to the rhythmic clip-clop of

EAST GARSTON – EASTBURY

The walk starts by the post office in the village of East Garston Ⓐ.

▶**1** Cross the bridge over the river and turn left. Continue following the road as it turns round to the right past Downlands.

▶**2** At Manor Farm continue straight on through the farmyard.

▶**3** Where the broad track swings round to the left, continue straight on uphill in the direction indicated by the footpath sign. Take great care as the footpath may have been planted over and may not be easy to follow.

▶**4** At the top of the hill cross the fence. This brings

▲*Local building materials are rare. Houses in Eastbury and East Garston are mostly timber-framed and brick.*

hooves as the strings of racehorses head to and from the downs.

Once past the farm, the special nature of the downland becomes apparent. The Downs were once part of a great dome of chalk that stretched not just across southern England but all the way to France. During the millions of years of geological time, the sea broke through to create the English Channel and rivers formed valleys that split up the downs into separate regions. Over the centuries, the soft chalk weathered, gently and slowly eroding to create the smooth curves, the

dips and hollows and the rounded hills that are such a feature of the region. This is a very open landscape, of wide vistas, but it is by no means an empty landscape.

At first the track runs through farmland. The soil is thin but modern agriculture, with its artificial fertilizers has made it possible to grow crops on it. The nature of that soil is particularly evident in winter, when it has a curious whitish tinge, created by the chalk and the flint nodules that can be seen scattered over the ground. The path climbs gently uphill, then dips down

towards Winterdown Bottom. The barn at the foot of the hill is home to a surprising occupant — not livestock, nor fodder, but a light aircraft.

Then the path climbs steeply over the last of the farmland to reach the grassland of the ridge that marks the high point of East Garston Down Ⓑ. Here are the gallops, marked out by a row of neat, numbered white posts which not only mark out the course but are used by trainers for timing

you into an area set out with steeplechase jumps **B**. Leave the jumps on your left and head for the stile.

5 At the stile turn left to follow the line of the fence.

6 Cross further stile. At the broad track, turn left.

7 At the farm, continue straight on, leaving farm buildings on your left, along the track marked 'By Way'.

8 At the far side of the copse, turn left onto the broad track with the copse on your left, then a group of conifers on your left.

Continue straight ahead for about 1½ miles (2.5 km).

9 At the edge of the village of Eastbury **C**, turn left to cross the stile by the footpath sign. Past the first house, go through the gate and turn right by the wire fence, cross the stile and

turn left. The path crosses a series of stiles and appears to go through gardens before joining the obvious track of the disused railway **D**.

10 Beyond the church, turn right to rejoin the road to return to the start.

---

the horses. Here too are practice fences. If you have never seen a steeplechase fence at close quarters, you may be surprised at both the height and depth of these daunting obstacles. It is obviously essential that walkers keep well clear of horses being put through their paces.

Horses do not have the downs to themselves. In spring, in particular,

◀Signposts are confusing but should not hinder the walk.

this is a good place for watching hares, which can sometimes be seen up on their hind legs 'boxing' with each other, and rabbits are even more common. The skylark is a popular resident, rising above the nesting ground with its clear warbling song. Where the skylark seems a solitary bird, the lapwing is altogether more gregarious and flocks of the birds, flashing their black and white plumage in the sun, add their 'peewit' cry to the downland air.

SPLENDID VIEWS

The path continues over the grassland, rising now altogether more gently as it goes. It is worth pausing occasionally to look back at the splendid views over the Lambourn Valley. At the top of the hill, the walk returns to farmland where in

▼The rolling open hills of the Berkshire Downs provide the perfect countryside to train racehorses.

winter and early spring the furrows of the plough accentuate the curves of the hills. The farm track leads on down to the farm of Eastbury Grange. The house itself sits comfortably in a little hollow, given extra shelter by a screen of trees, while the farm buildings are spread out around it. Just beyond the farm is a small copse, a narrow finger of

▲You would be very unlucky to make it right round the walk without seeing at least one horse.

trees that points away south down the hillside. It seems a meagre covering of woodland, but it is enough to provide a home for the local deer population. Sometimes, they are surprised by walkers and go dashing off across the fields showing their distinctive white rumps.

VILLAGES

The broad track dips then rises steeply to the high point of the downs before descending steadily to the village of Eastbury **C**. Eastbury itself is, not surprisingly, similar in character to neighbouring East Garston. Again, it is based on a main village street running along the

The History of Horse Racing

Horse racing goes back to antiquity — at least as far as the chariot races of Greece and Rome — but racing as we know it in Britain dates back to the Stuart kings. It was James I who established stables at Newmarket where he kept racehorses and 'riders for the races' — the first royal jockeys. By the end of the 17th century racecourses had spread around the country, and breeders began introducing Arabian stock. Three of these stallions were

stables were established for training the horses. Suitable regions needed to have extensive areas of open grassland over which gallops could be laid for practice. The Berkshire Downs proved ideal for the purpose. The flinty, chalky soil was considered too poor for ploughing, but once the trees had been cleared it developed as springy turf, used for grazing. Stables were developed in the villages of the Lambourn Valley and each day horses are led up to

▲ *Steeplechasing is also practised on the Downs. The size of the fences appears daunting to the walker.*

KIT HOUGHTON

The rolling chalk downlands of Berkshire make the perfect exercise and training ground for racehorses.

the sires from which all 'thoroughbreds' are descended.

Racing developed as a sport in two broad categories: flat racing and racing over jumps — either the high fences of the steeplechase or the less demanding hurdles. Special

gallops such as those of Winterdown for exercise and training over the jumps.

So-called modern training methods were introduced in the 1840s. Before that horses were taken on long gallops, swathed in heavy rugs to make them sweat. Today's trainers are more scientific, choosing the training methods best suited to each individual horse.

a former railway **D**, as becomes abundantly clear once you are quite clear of the houses.

The Lambourn Valley Railway was begun in 1898 under the Light Railway Act. This allowed for railways being built on the cheap, to lower standards than those that applied to their bigger brethren.

SAFETY FACTORS

Safety factors were less stringently applied, but there was a price to be paid in slower trains and poorer service. Thanks to the Act, however, many regions were served by railways which would otherwise have been denied them, and the little Lambourn Valley Railway was, for a time, a real boon to the horse-racing community. It could not, however, compete with the motor car and the horse box. Sadly, the line closed in 1960. Much of the character of the line is, however, still clear.

River Lambourn, and again the older houses and cottages are timber-framed with thatched roofs. Some of the larger barns have now been converted into private houses. The walk itself runs rather curiously, through the gardens of houses, but it is nevertheless a public right-of-way. Walkers, however, must be sure to follow the signs and cross fences by the stiles. Near the beginning, the path passes a field on the left, and it is worth pausing to look at the iron gateposts. These are a distinctive shape in cross-section – Ω – and they

were originally railway track. They were used on the old Great Western Railway in the days when it was broad gauge, with rails set 7 feet (2.1 metres) apart instead of the standard 4 ft 8½ ins (1.4 metres) in use on the rest of the system and used throughout Britain today. You can also see an old goods wagon in use as a store in the fields. In fact this footpath is following the line of

▶ *It is traditional for racing stables to have a weather vane in the shape of a horse. This is a splendid variation.*

ALL PHOTOS ROB SCOTT

ROLLING CHALK DOWNLAND

Over windswept downs, through sheltered valleys and woodlands

This walk is through typical downland countryside. At one time, much of southern England consisted of a great dome of chalk that through the long ages of geological time was gradually broken up and shaped by the weather. The River Kennet now divides this section of chalk hills from the Berkshire Downs to the north. Here the north-facing slope of Inkpen Hill drops away in a steep escarpment, while to the south the countryside has been more gently moulded into a

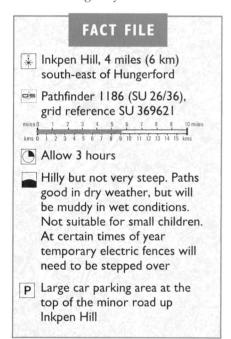

FACT FILE

* Inkpen Hill, 4 miles (6 km) south-east of Hungerford

os Pathfinder 1186 (SU 26/36), grid reference SU 369621

miles 0 1 2 3 4 5 6 7 8 9 10 miles
kms 0 1 2 3 4 5 6 7 8 9 10 11 12 13 14 15 kms

◔ Allow 3 hours

▬ Hilly but not very steep. Paths good in dry weather, but will be muddy in wet conditions. Not suitable for small children. At certain times of year temporary electric fences will need to be stepped over

P Large car parking area at the top of the minor road up Inkpen Hill

ROB SCOTT. INSET:ALAN BARNES/NHPA

landscape of softly curving hills that swoop down to sheltered hollows.

From the ridge you can look down on just such a hollow, in which a farm sits snugly protected from the weather. The path leads on along the edge of the escarpment and at once passes through a gap that marks the entrance to the Iron Age hill fort of Walbury Hill Ⓐ. The way leads through to the centre of the old fortress, now occupied by fields of grain, and emerges by a small stand of beech.

▲*Sheltering in a wooded hollow of the Berkshire downlands lies Wright's Farm. The holly blue butterfly (inset) is seen in hedgerows from March to October and breeds twice a year.*

The path now leaves the broad track of the escarpment, with its shiny nodules of flint, for coarse grassland dotted with gorse. An old hollow way, sunk deep into the hill and sheltered by trees, leads down from the wide, windswept expanses of the downs to the valley. There it

joins another broad track shaded by large, mature trees. It brings you out at the hamlet of Combe Ⓑ.

The attraction of tiny villages such as this derive in good measure from their intimate relationship to the country around them. There is no good building stone here, but the clay of the valley can be used for brick-making; there is timber in the woods and everywhere one can see the hard nodules of flint in the ground. So you can see walls of flint, reinforced by bands of brick;

THE WALK

GALLOWS DOWN – COMBE – INKPEN HIILL

The walk starts at the car park at the top of Gallows Down.

1 Facing out towards Inkpen and the valley, turn right along the footpath signposted 'Wayfarers Walk'. It passes through the ramparts of Walbury Hill fort **A**.

2 On the far side of the hill fort is a stand of beech trees. Just beyond the trees leave the broad track and turn right, by the sign with the yellow arrow marked 'Public Footpath'. Head for the left-hand side of the small wood, down the hill and here join a hollow way and follow it down hill to a signpost marked 'By Way'.

3 Here turn right and follow the by way down to Combe **B**.

4 At the road junction, turn left along Church Lane, signposted Linkenholt and Netherton.

5 Where the road swings sharply round to the left, following a right-hand bend with warning chevrons, continue straight on up the broad track in the hollow way, past the church and the farm, signposted 'By Way'. Do not turn onto the left-hand track here.

6 At the top of the hill beyond a point where a conspicuous farm track crosses the path, at the far edge of a little copse, go through the farm gate on your right and head diagonally leftwards across the field as indicated by the sign Public Footpath.

7 Skirting the left-hand edge of the nearest part of the wood, at the far side of the field, leave the field by the makeshift wooden gate in the far corner. Enter the wood **C**, following the footpath shown by the white arrow (on the right-hand post of an opening in the wire fence on the left). The woods are private and walkers must keep to the clearly signposted footpath.

8 At the far edge of the wood, cross the broad track bordering it and go over the stile, across the wire fence in front, to head downhill towards the woods on the opposite side of the valley, passing the left-hand end of a new fenced plantation some way down the hill and not visible from the stile.

9 Turn 'half-right' on the first track below the bottom stile and continue down to the bottom of the valley and then up the track seen from above that curves round beside the edge of the woodland. Continue following this track to Buttermere. In its middle section the track surface is entirely of grass. Ignore the prominent track on the left, turning into the wood and keep straight on.

10 At the road turn right.

11 At the road junction, turn right on the road marked as a dead end. This continues as a track that swings round to the left.

12 Do not turn through the gate in front, but turn right on to the broad track along the edge of the downs and follow this past Combe Gibbet **D** to return to the start.

weather-boarding can be added or tiles hung on a gable end. Roofs can be thatch or bright red tiles.

The other centre of life here is the old manor house and the church, reached along narrow Church Lane, which runs between high banks topped by mature beech trees. The church of St Swithin is a simple but very attractive little building with flint walls and a timber tower. The porch bears the date 1652, but the church is much older than that, begun in 1160, and it is well worth a visit. Inside the church, on the nave floor, is a group of 17th-century tombstones, each engraved with a coat of arms and the simple font has

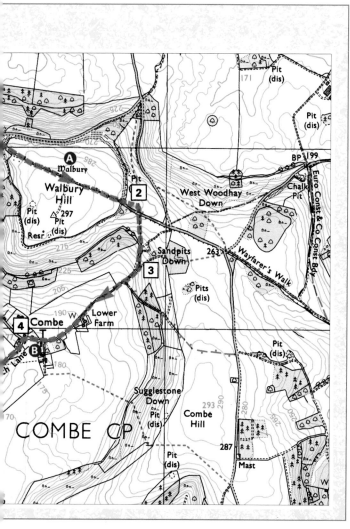

▲*On the high downlands, hollows were dug to provide sheep with dew and rain water.*

▶*Combe Gibbet, built for the purpose of hanging, has stood on Inkpen Hill since 1676.*

ALL PHOTOS ROB SCOTT

a Saxon bowl resting on a medieval base. One of the bells in the tower was cast in 1430. Next to the church is Manor Farm on the site of the old manor house, surrounded by a high wall with a rather attractive gazebo in the corner.

▲*This cottage in Combe is built from local materials — the flint walls with bands of brick are typical of the area.*

The walk now leaves the road for another broad track. Its banks are again topped by trees, but now birch rather than beech predominates and, beneath the branches, the green of grass and moss is speckled with wild flowers — it is particularly attractive in spring when primroses are in bloom. The path itself has reached through the top soil to the chalk, so that while it is firm and pleasant underfoot in fine weather, it becomes slimy in the wet.

CHANGING LANDSCAPES

As you climb, so the view opens out, back to the neat, comfortable buildings of Manor Farm, surrounded by its parkland, and back across to Walbury Hill, where the deep 'V' of the ditch is prominent on the horizon. As the hill begins to level out, so the track becomes less of a deep-cut way and takes on the character of a green lane, and there is a more open feel to the walk as you make your way through farmland. It is,

however, only an interlude — for you soon leave the track to head downhill towards Combe Wood **C**.

The nature of this woodland becomes obvious even before you enter it. You leave the field by the side of a patch of maize grown to feed the wood's valuable inhabitants. They make themselves heard long before you see them, for above the hollow, hoo-hooing call of the wood pigeons comes the harsher voice of the pheasant. The woods are well maintained and coppiced, but their primary purpose these days is to provide a home for game birds. The tall cylinders to be seen in

Downland Burial Sites

Downland escarpments have a special significance in ancient history: they provided a very useful means of crossing the country on a route that was literally high and dry, in contrast to the soft clays and dense forests of the valley. The section of this walk that runs from Ham Hill in the west to Walbury Hill in the east has been used by travellers for thousands of years. Unlike later road builders, they left no physical traces to remind us of their journeys.

The people who settled in the area, however, have left two splendid monuments, the oldest of which dates from the New Stone Age that lasted from roughly 4000 to 2000 BC. This is the long barrow at Combe Gibbet. It appears now as a grassy mound, 66 yards (60 metres) long and 2.2 yards (2 metres) high, with ditches at either side, the one on the downhill side being the easier to see. The people of that time kept their dead in mortuary houses, then at some suitable time the bodies were brought together for communal burial. Turfs were dug to cover the bodies, and the huge mounds surrounded by wooden walls, which have now decayed.

The next monument, Walbury Hill fort, brings us forward to the Iron Age, which began around 500 BC and lasted until the Roman occupation. The country was occupied by Celtic people, much prone to tribal warfare. As a result, communities expended a great deal of effort on building fortresses. Walbury is a typical hill fort taking advantage of the natural defence afforded by the hill. The flat plateau has been surrounded by earthwork defences. A deep ditch was dug all around the summit, and the material from it piled up to create a rampart.

A funeral ceremony during the New Stone Age when bodies were buried in long barrows, an example of which can be found at Combe Gibbet on top of Inkpen Hill.

the woods supply grain for feed. It is very important that walkers keep to the public paths through the woods. Once clear of Combe Wood, the path takes to the fields again and you find an interesting mixture of woodland dotting the gently rolling hills: old coppiced woodland alternates with newer conifer plantations and here and there small groups stand out. One group of trees might be notable for the clamorous rookery that occupies the topmost branches, palely slender silver birch stand close to the pathway and on the horizon there are occasional glimpses of tall majestic pine. The combination of grassy slopes, fields of grain and a splendid mixture of woodland makes this a particularly

▶ *Viewed from the highest point in Berkshire, the pattern of tractor tracks in the field exposes the chalky soil.*

▲*This traditonal thatched wooden barn is elevated by stone mushrooms to protect the harvest from vermin.*

attractive landscape. This part of the walk ends at Buttermere, where it first passes the simple little flint church that nestles in a hollow and is overwhelmed by yew trees. This is an even more scattered settlement than Combe.

HANGMAN'S GALLOWS

The final part of the walk follows a path along the edge of the escarpment, which offers wide views over the Kennet valley. Shortly you reach the high point of Gallows Down, with its Neolithic long barrow. The prehistoric burial site is not the only point of interest here: rearing up above it is the sombre shape of Combe Gibbet ❿. The Lord of Combe Manor had an ancient right to condemn felons to death, without the accused having any right to trial. If the lord declared them guilty they were brought to this lonely spot and hung, after which their bodies were left as a grim warning to others.

ROB SCOTT. INSET: S.C. BROWN/AQUILA

Through broadleaved woodland and alongside the River Pang

T he walk is mainly on footpaths over fields and through broad-leaved woods, and includes visits to two delightful villages. The walk starts in the middle of woodland, of a type which is to feature for much of the way. Oak and birch dominate, while the forest floor carries a dense covering of ferns, among which a variety of sometimes large and colourful fungi can be seen.

WOODLAND GLADES

At the beginning the track is broad and gravelly, but soon changes to a narrower green path through the trees. In general the woodland is quite dense, but every now and then it opens out into attractive glades. At the junction of the tracks is a small thatch and timber cottage.

The track leaves the woodland temporarily to give wide vistas over

tree-covered hills and fields of grain. Although out of the wood, the path is still shaded by oak trees and cottages can be glimpsed almost lost from sight among the greenery. For a while, crop fields, their margins

▲ *The church in Bucklebury is built of flint with a red-tiled roof. The turtle dove (inset) is a summer visitor from sub-tropical Africa. It will often be seen around farm buildings feeding on grain.*

bright with poppies, adjoin the path before it dips into a dense copse Ⓐ.

This tiny area of woodland seems almost to be bursting with wildlife: squirrels rush around the branches and the copse echoes with bird cries. Apart from the ubiquitous wood pigeon, you can spot jay, nuthatch, the tiny goldcrest and a great many more species. The birds flit to and fro across the tree-shaded path, while partridge and pheasant can be glimpsed in the adjoining fields.

THISTLES AND ROSES

Beyond the copse, trees have been felled to create a rough area of wasteland where a variety of plants flourish, including thistles which grow well above head height. The path dodges back into a narrow lane bordered by dog roses that brings you down to the road and the

THE WALK

BUCKLEBURY COMMON – BUCKLEBURY – STANFORD DINGLEY

The walk starts near Bucklebury Common at the crossroads where the Bucklebury and Upper Bucklebury roads meet.

1 Turn down the road signposted to Bucklebury village, and after 80 yards (73 metres) turn left onto the broad track through the woods.

2 Where the tracks cross near a small clearing turn right.

3 At the junction of the tracks turn right.

4 Where the path divides by an iron gate, continue straight on along the path through the edge of the copse **A**. At the far side of the copse continue straight on, keeping the narrow strip of woodland on your right.

5 At the road turn right and on to Bucklebury church **B**. Take the footpath through the churchyard to the tower and bear left through two kissing gates and across the field to a field gate and another kissing gate. Cross the bridge over the River Pang (the river is just a dry ditch for many months of the year).

6 At the road junction turn right. There are fine views across the broad Pang valley.

7 At the entrance to Rushdens Farm turn right onto the blue waymarked bridleway.

8 At the river turn left. Do not cross the bridge but follow the path along the side of the Pang.

9 Just before the chalk pit, turn right as indicated by the yellow arrow. The path then divides: turn left as indicated by the yellow arrow. Cross the field, leaving the new plantation on your left, to go through the woodland and head towards the church.

10 At the road turn right into Stanford Dingley **C** and opposite the Bull Inn take the footpath, between the seats and the wooden fence, past the old mill. Turn right onto the road.

11 Just before the thatched cottage, turn left onto the green lane shaded by trees. At the gate continue straight on as indicated by the blue arrow. Ignore the stile to the right.

12 At the road turn right. Just before the little pond, turn left onto the path, leaving the prominent oak tree on your left, then bear left to follow the path that cuts through the woodland.

13 At the broad gravel track turn left. There are many tracks through the woods, but keep to the path that follows the power lines strung on tall wooden poles, back to the crossroads at the start of the walk.

village of Bucklebury, close by the church **B**. The latter, with an attractive timber-framed house bordering the churchyard, is worth a detour.

The walk now follows the road as it winds and twists through the little village, past the 'Victory Room' at the edge of the cricket field, the post office and the very attractive Riverside Cottages, with old and very tiny lattice windows. Here the River Pang is no more than a gently trickling stream, but it will grow to become an important tributary of the Thames at Pangbourne.

The road continues its circuitous way through the village, crossing the Pang on a simple brick bridge, before heading off towards an impressive stand of pine at the crossroads, where it turns to follow a route parallel to the Pang. The riverside fields are full of pigs foraging, while close by the water is an immense wooden barn with prominent porches.

RIVER PANG

The walk now turns off the road and back onto footpaths, starting with a deep, sunken lane, with a bank topped by a thick-set thorn hedge on one side and mature trees on the

◀Soft green ferns lie under delicate birch trees by this footpath, which runs through the woods near the start of the walk. Fungi grow among the ferns.

▶Stalks of barley, ready for harvest, are seen in the foreground. Behind lies arable farmland and woodland that is close to the village of Bucklebury.

other. This lane leads down to the Pang, which at this stage is still little more than a winding stream, overhung with willows. The lane follows the stream before cutting across the fields towards Stanford Dingley **C**. It goes through another patch of woodland, then heads across a field where the bumps and hollows suggest clay has been dug out for brick-making for the local buildings. It then arrives at the road and the church at Stanford Dingley.

VILLAGE ARCHITECTURE

This church is rather more conventional than that at Bucklebury. Its main body is flint with a brick extension and it has a timber tower and slate-clad steeple. Only the moat of the old neighbouring manor house now remains, out of sight, behind the walls of Manor Farm.

The village itself, however, turns out to have many buildings of great character and charm. The first building of note is the 15th-century Bull Inn, which looks out across the village green. It has an unusual sign: on one side is the conventional head-on view of a bull, but the reverse shows only his backside.

The village houses show a mixture of building materials. There are bricks, often set in a diamond pattern, with blue headers alternating with dark red stretchers to create a chequerboard pattern. There is also weatherboarding and walls hung with tiles in intricate patterns.

From the bridge over the river you can see the converted village

Nature Walk

BLACKBIRD NESTS are made of grass and lined with mud; they are found in the fork of a tree or shrub.

WREN NESTS are dome-shaped and lined with feathers; they are built into tree hollows, from ground level up.

mill, but the grandest houses appear after you have turned the corner towards Bucklebury Common. A timber-framed cottage stands next to a thoroughly urbane Georgian house. The name 'Garden House' is amply justified, for the formal gardens across the road

◀The 15th-century rose- and ivy-covered Bull Inn in Stanford Dingley offers refreshment on the walk.

Bucklebury Church

Even at a first glance, the church and churchyard are full of interesting and unusual features. The walls and tower are of flint, but the roof is of red tile into which a prominent dormer window has been let, giving it an oddly domestic appearance. In the graveyard, among the conventional stones, are a number of cast-iron headstones.

The entrance is through a 12th-century doorway, with carved heads above the arch and once inside, it is soon obvious that the interior lives up to expectation. Box pews fill the nave and the reason for the dormer window appears — to provide light for the balcony, emblazoned with the names of benefactors.

Restoration has been sympathetic and the one prominent Victorian window at the east end is at least full of colour and vitality — the work of the artist Frank Brangwyn. But by far the most interesting window can be found just behind the plush-lined pew, set aside for the squire. On it is a stained-glass sundial, alongside which is a meticulously painted and completely realistic fly. One other monument deserves special mention — on the wall opposite the door is a bas-relief by the respected 20th-century carver and typographer Eric Gill, who is famous for his stone and wood carvings.

This stained-glass window in Bucklebury church depicts a sundial. An attempt at realism is seen in the painted fly on the left.

▲*In early summer the blue flowers of bugle, a plant valued by herbalists, are found among the woodland of this area.*

would not disgrace the grandest country mansion. The house has a formal 18th-century frontage, but the gable end has tiles hung in regular, but complex, patterns. Beyond the 18th-century Boot Inn is an attractive timber-framed house with traditional cottage garden, but beyond that is the grandest of all the old village houses, the Old Rectory. Those with a taste for English domestic architecture may well wish to wander on to the outskirts of the village, where there are still more delights to discover, but the walk itself turns off to return to footpaths, fields and woods.

This section begins with a deep lane, shaded by trees, which emerges into a field bounded by woodland. Up ahead a long line of poplars, planted as a wind break, dominates the horizon. Beyond this is a very extensive orchard. The path arrives at the road by an attractive thatched cottage, but soon turns off again to head back into the woods.

It is said that the parish of Bucklebury has more footpaths than any other in England and meeting the maze of paths this is not difficult to believe. Fortunately, a procession of poles carrying power lines serves as a guide for the rest of the walk.

AN ANCIENT COMMON

The rest of the walk leads over Bucklebury Common, which is recorded in the Domesday Book as Borgeldeberie Hundred (the land of Burghild's Fort). It was once a royal hunting ground and in 1644, some 20,000 Parliamentary troops camped out in the woods here before the Battle of Newbury.

Today, this wooded area is enjoyed for peaceful recreation. It remains predominantly oak and beech, and a large area of young trees along the way provides evidence of the efforts being made to preserve this ancient woodland. The common is enjoyed by many long-distance hikers and dog-walkers. The path stays in the confines of the woods until the end of the walk.

▼*The 18th-century frontage of the Garden House in Stanford Dingley. The fine, formal garden verifies its name.*

BOTH PHOTOS ROB SCOTT

P. CLEMENT/BRUCE COLEMAN LTD

DAVID HUGHES. INSET: E.A. JANES/NHPA

An historic castle and a famous college by the Thames

Along this attractive stretch of the River Thames, there are good views of Windsor Castle and Eton College. There are busy reaches, with a variety of craft to be observed, as well as quiet back-waters where you may be tempted to relax for a while.

WREN'S JEST

The walk starts on Windsor Bridge, built in 1824 and now closed to traffic. Nearby is Wren's House **Ⓐ**. Sir Christopher Wren stayed here while supervising the building of the Guildhall in 1690. The town corporation did not believe that the open ground floor would support the structure above, and insisted on additional columns. Wren complied, but left a small gap between the top

---

FACT FILE

☀ Windsor, 20 miles (32km) west of London

▭ Pathfinder 1173 (SU 87/97), grid reference SU 967772

miles 0 1 2 3 4 5 6 7 8 9 10 miles
kms 0 1 2 3 4 5 6 7 8 9 10 11 12 13 14 15 kms

◔ Allow 2½ hours

▬ Suitable for all seasons

Ⓟ Several car parks in Windsor; the nearest is the station car park, 200 yards (180m) from the start

Ⓣ Regular trains and buses from London and elsewhere

▦ Pubs, restaurants and cafés in Eton and Windsor

⊔ Windsor Castle Precincts open daily. East Terrace is closed when the Queen is in residence. Admission free

---

▲ *Windsor Castle dominates the town and the River Thames, which follows a winding path separating Windsor from Eton. The orange tip butterfly (inset) is commonly seen in May and June.*

of the columns and the ceiling in order to prove his point.

Above you is the fortified palace of Windsor Castle **Ⓑ**, surmounted by its conspicuous Round Tower. When the Queen is in residence, the Royal Standard is flown from its turret.

SWAN-UPPING

The riverside path leads to Romney Lock **Ⓒ**, site of the famous annual 'swan-upping' ceremony. The swans of the upper Thames are counted and marked by their owners — the Crown, and the Dyers' and Vintners' Companies of the City of London.

From the lock, there is a good view of Eton College Chapel **Ⓓ**, which is an outstanding example of the 15th-century Perpendicular style of architecture. Eton College was

THE WALK

WINDSOR – ETON WICK

The walk begins from Windsor Bridge.

1 From Windsor Bridge turn south, with Wren's House **Ⓐ** on your right, towards the castle **Ⓑ**. Descend a flight of steps on your left to a road beside the river. Follow this for 200 yards (180m) then, beside the station car park, take the riverside path through an iron gate. By a footbridge over the railway, it joins a road. Continue to where the road ends at a boatyard, then bear left to Romney Lock **Ⓒ** for a fine view of Eton College Chapel **Ⓓ**.

2 Do not cross the bridge, but turn right to a stile onto a path by the river. Follow the path under the arch of a railway bridge and along the edge of The Home Park. By a slight bend in the river, 100 yards (90m) before another bridge, turn right and go through a white-painted iron gate. Turn left along the road and cross the Victoria Bridge.

3 After 100 yards (90m), turn left through a gate onto Datchet golf course. Follow the gravel track and, when this becomes a grassy path, continue ahead beside a backwater of the river to the far end of the golf course, passing to the left of the final tee. Follow the path through willows and keep left at a fork to pass beneath the arch of a railway bridge. Go through the swing gate beyond, into a field. Cross this field, heading slightly left, and go over a small concrete bridge and a stile into a

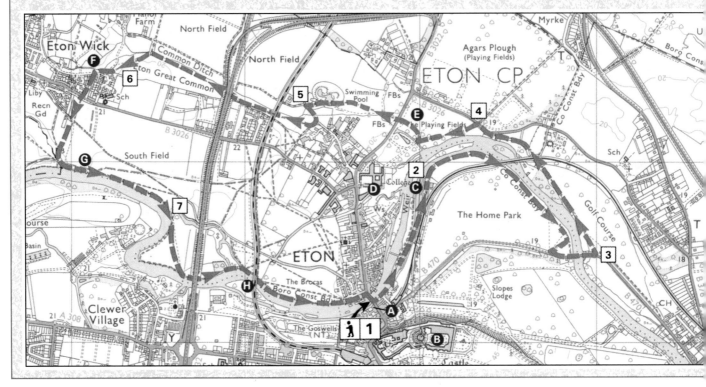

▼ *Windsor Bridge, now open only to pedestrians, links Eton with Windsor and is crossed at the end of the walk.*

DAVID HUGHES

founded by Henry VI in 1440, to train men to run the church and the state. Over the centuries it has supplied 18 prime ministers, as well as numerous bishops. It was the king's wish to build a church of cathedral-like proportions, and the chapel was to have been the chancel of a larger church. When Henry VI was deposed, the plans were shelved.

RETURN OF THE SALMON

Beyond the lock, a quiet stretch of the river has been developed as a fishery. Salmon were absent from the polluted Thames for over 150 years, but now that the river is cleaner, the salmon have returned. Salmon 'ladders' have been built at the weirs, to allow the fish to reach their breeding grounds in the tributaries of the river. The fields near here are particularly attractive to butterflies in summer. Herons and kingfishers may both be seen catching fish in the Thames here.

After passing beneath the railway, the route crosses The Home Park, which belongs to the castle. This and the adjoining Windsor Great Park measure 6 miles (9.6km) from north to south, and comprise some 5,000 acres (2,000ha). This vast area was used by the king and his court for deer-hunting.

The route crosses the Victoria Bridge, built in 1851. From here there is a superb view of the castle

lane. Turn left and very soon, at a gate onto a private bridge, turn right along a footpath beside a backwater. Pass in front of a large boathouse, then through a gate and turn left along the road.

4 After a few paces, turn left on a path over a bridge into Eton College playing fields ❷. Follow the clear path across the fields towards a brick-built bridge, with Eton College visible beyond. Just before the bridge, turn right along a path leading to a lodge, now used as a cricket pavilion. Continue across the road to a gate in the fence opposite and onto a path across another playing field, then enter a third field. Follow the path beside a stream to the far left corner, then through a small wood. Go past the college's swimming pool and along a short drive to come to a road.

5 Turn left, and 50 yards (45m) beyond a bridge over a stream, turn right through a wooden gate beside a wall, into a field. Keeping to the left side of the field, follow it around two sides

to pass under the railway viaduct. Continue on the grassy path alongside Common Ditch, passing beneath a road-bridge, then through a gate into a large field, Eton Great Common. Keeping the watercourse on your right, go to the far end of the common and then go through a gate onto a road.

6 Turn right and follow the road round a bend to The Greyhound pub ❻. Turn left along a road. At the T-junction go right and immediately left along the signposted footpath. Continue across a large field to a path alongside the Thames. Turn left along the bank, passing the memorial stone of the Athens Bathing Place ❼, and continue until you come to a footbridge.

7 Cross the bridge over a stream and follow the clear path beyond it. When it rejoins the river, continue beneath the road-bridge, then the railway bridge ❽. When the path ends beside the college boathouses, go through a gate and continue ahead to Eton High Street, turning right to Windsor Bridge where you started.

ALL PHOTOS: DAVID HUGHES

▲ *A statue of Eton College's founder, the pious Henry VI, stands in front of Lupton's Tower at Eton. Henry also founded King's College, Cambridge.*

age of 15. The route continues towards the North Lodge cricket pavilion, with views of the bend in the river towards Eton Weir and the college buildings beyond.

The path enters other college fields, passing the college swimming pool and the now-obsolete assault course. The willow-lined Common Ditch flows across Eton

and its grounds. The path along the edge of Datchet golf course passes beside a quiet, tree-shaded backwater of the main river. The next field beyond the railway line contains many teasels, which were once used widely for brushing and raising the nap of woollen cloth.

Next, the path crosses the playing fields ❷ of Eton College. They are famous for the remark made by the Duke of Wellington that the Battle of Waterloo was won on them. The 'Iron Duke' himself left Eton at the

◀ *The Home Park lies in a bend of the Thames. On its west side is Romney Lock (right) where, in July, swan-uppers notch the bills of young swans.*

▲*As well as offering a drink, The Greyhound has a skittle alley. The game has been played in pubs for centuries.*

Great Common, which is still used for cattle-grazing. At Eton Wick, The Greyhound pub ❻ retains an old-fashioned 10-pin skittle alley in a separate low building. A field path crosses South Field to the Thames. Windsor racecourse is situated on the large island across the river.

TOWARDS THE CASTLE

Downstream, towards the distant castle, a memorial stone on the bank marks the site of the Athens Bathing Place ❼, a swimming spot once popular with boys from Eton College. Beyond the road-bridge is a great iron-girder railway bridge ❽ that

▼*Many mute swans frequent this stretch of the Thames. Those with unnotched bills belong to the Crown.*

ALL PHOTOS: DAVID HUGHES

has recently been restored. It was over this bridge that dignitaries were once transported by train to Windsor. The railway station and royal train have been restored, and dozens of life-size wax models of guardsmen, together with the royal party headed by Queen Victoria, wait to greet modern visitors.

Just short of Eton College boat-house is a bank, often occupied by a flock of swans. From here, there is another impressive view of the castle, which towers above the town on its promontory. A lane leads past the ancient Waterman's Arms pub to Eton High Street and Windsor Bridge where the walk began.

Windsor Castle

Windsor, a favourite residence of Queen Elizabeth II, is the largest inhabited castle in the world, occupying a site of 13 acres (5.3ha).

Together with the Tower of London, it was a stronghold of the Norman kings, and it provided a base from which to hunt in the royal forest of Windsor. The original castle was built by William the Conqueror in about 1070. It had a timber palisade, built upon a huge, man-made earth mound. The Round Tower was begun by Henry II on the original mound. It was increased to its present height much later by George IV, in 1828. Henry III (1216-1272) added the Salisbury, Garter and Curlew Towers.

In the 14th century, during the reign of Edward III, the castle was extended to house a series of royal apartments. Windsor became a centre for the King's Order of the Garter, the first of several European orders of chivalry. Based on the 'round table' of Arthurian legend, its original purpose was to provide a company of 300 knights. Evidence suggests that the Order was inaugurated at a tournament held at Windsor in 1348, when two teams of 12 knights, one commanded by Edward III and the other by the Black Prince, wore a distinctive badge that gave the order its name.

The building of the present Royal Chapel was started by Edward IV (1460-1483) and completed in the reign of Henry VIII. Ten monarchs are buried there.

During the Civil War, the town of Windsor opened its gates to the Parliamentary army, and it was at the castle that the Army Council met, and decided to prosecute Charles I for his life. Following his execution, he was buried in St George's Chapel. After the Restoration of the

The Norman Gate at Windsor Castle. Begun shortly after the Norman Conquest, the castle became a royal residence in Henry I's reign. Much of it dates from the 19th century.

Monarchy in 1660, Charles II enjoyed Windsor to the full. He swam and sculled on the river, and played tennis in his newly-built courts. His mistress, Nell Gwynne, lived in the town at Burford House.

During the reign of George IV (1820-1830), the castle underwent profound restoration. In all, some £800,000 was spent, and the castle today owes its appearance to him.

In 1839, Queen Victoria first met Albert, the future Prince Consort, here. They spent their honeymoon in the castle, and he died in 1861 in its Blue Room.

At Fort Belvedere, in Windsor's grounds, the future Edward VIII held weekend parties at which Mrs Wallis Simpson was often a guest. In 1936, the king broadcast his abdication speech to the nation from his old rooms in the Augusta Tower.

SUE MORRIS. INSET: PAUL STERRY/NATURE PHOTOGRAPHERS

Discover the fascinating history of a downland village

The ancient village of East Ilsley is a pleasant base from which to explore the Berkshire Downs and the Ridgeway. Exhilarating views of the surrounding countryside are in easy reach, and the bracing air quickly blows away the cobwebs.

Some believe that the hill south of East Ilsley was the site of the Battle of Ashdown in AD871, where the invading Danes were defeated by King Aethelred and his brother (later King Alfred). The Saxons called the area 'Hildes-Laeg', or 'battlefield', and it is from this name that Ilsley is derived.

In the 14th century, the manor here passed to the Duchy of Lancaster and the family of Henry IV. Major sheep fairs were held regularly in the town, and at least ten inns catered for the influx of people on market days. One of these is the Swan Inn **Ⓐ**, where the walk starts. The present building dates

▲*From the Ridgeway there are views in all directions over the Berkshire Downs. The Devil's coach horse beetle (inset), often found near horse dung, preys on other insects and spiders.*

FACT FILE

☀ East Ilsley, 9½ miles (15.2km) north of Newbury, off the A34

🗺 Pathfinder 1155 (SU 48/58), grid reference SU 492811

miles 0 1 2 3 4 5 6 7 8 9 10 miles
kms 0 1 2 3 4 5 6 7 8 9 10 11 12 13 14 15 kms

◔ Allow 1½ hours

⬛ Well marked footpaths and bridleways. A long, steady but gentle climb from the village to the Ridgeway. Children and dogs should be kept off the gallops

Ⓟ On street, or use the Swan Inn's car park if patronizing the public house

Ⓣ For details of local buses, Tel. (01635) 40743

🍺 Three pubs in East Ilsley

SUE MORRIS

from the 17th century, and was used to quarter some of Charles I's army when he dined at nearby Compton.

In the 18th century, East Ilsley became famous for its thorough-breds, and the celebrated Eclipse was stabled nearby. Racehorses are still trained here to this day; the route passes by Summerdown Stables **Ⓑ**, then runs alongside a gallop to the top of the downs.

▼*Leaving East Ilsley, the path runs parallel to gallops where thoroughbred racehorses are exercised at first light.*

THE WALK

EAST ILSLEY – RIDGEWAY PATH

The walk begins outside the Swan Inn **A**.

1 With your back to the inn's car park, turn right and go straight ahead at the junction. You pass a chapel on your left and a pond on your right. As you leave the village, turn left at the waymark by the entrance to Summerdown Stables **B**.

2 At the top of the gallops, turn right on the Ridgeway **C**. Continue past a farm access lane on the right, to a crossroads.

3 Turn right and follow the byway downhill, to a road at the bottom.

4 Cross and continue on the path ahead. At the first path junction, turn right. By East Ilsley's first houses, take a path left, up the field and around some gardens. You emerge opposite St Mary's Church **D**.

5 Turn right down the road. Take the first left, and turn right at the T-junction. Pen Meadow **E** is on the left, and the Swan Inn is about 100 yards (90m) ahead.

The route meets the Ridgeway **C**, which lays claim to the title of the oldest road in Britain. The high, dry chalk ridge that runs from the Chilterns across the downland of Berkshire and Wiltshire formed a natural trackway for early settlers, and must have been used as a route to and from the prehistoric religious centres at Stonehenge and Avebury.

ANCIENT TRADE

The Ridgeway was also a trade route; flint axes and arrowheads were brought along it in the Stone Age, and gold ornaments and copper and bronze tools in the Bronze Age. Many Iron Age hill forts were built along its length.

The Romans, however, do not appear to have made much use of

▼*The duckpond in the village of East Ilsley is home to various hybrid ducks.*

the route, and the Ridgeway declined into obscurity. Farms and villages sprang up in the valleys below the scarp slope. The roads that grew up to connect them took over from the Ridgeway, which was higher and less convenient. In the Middle Ages, it was used by drovers to avoid turnpike tolls. This was one of the reasons that East Ilsley developed as a sheep market. Today, the oldest road has been revived as a walkers' path.

The route follows the Ridgeway, from which there are wonderful views of the downs to the north, and of the ancient tumuli that dot the hilltops. The cooling towers of Didcot Power Station are a landmark visible for many miles around.

The hedgerows are a delight in summer, with many species of chalk-loving plants in colourful flower. Look for harebells and

knapweed, toadflax and melilot, betony and red bartsia, meadow cranesbill and chicory, restharrow and wild mignonette. Chalkhill blue and meadow brown butterflies may be spotted, and the song of skylarks is a continuous accompaniment to the walk. During the winter months, flocks of black and white lapwings can be seen flying overhead.

Back in East Ilsley, the Church of St Mary **D** is worth a visit. The first church on this ancient site was probably built in the early 11th century; it is mentioned in the *Domesday Book*. In 1199, King John gave the church to the Knights Hospitallers. In about 1240, it was much enlarged, and additions and alterations have been made down the centuries. The oldest remaining part is the south arcade. The interior walls incline outwards, an indication of their great age. The heads of a monk and nun at each end of the chancel arch were carved in the 15th century.

PEN MEADOW

On your way back to the Swan Inn, you pass Pen Meadow **E**, the site of the famous East Ilsley sheep fairs, which, at one time, were second in importance only to Smithfield. They were held fortnightly from April to October. The last fair was held in 1934, but the local residents still hold an annual country fair on the same site, creating a link with the past of this pretty village.

SUE MORRIS

◀ A quiet country scene near Farnborough. Each flower head of the colourful lady orchid (inset) resembles a lady in a dress.

DEREK PRATT. INSET: E A JAMES/NHPA

A pleasant rural walk just a few moments away from suburban London

To walk from the centre of Farnborough down Church Road is to step from London's suburbia into leafy country lanes within just a few paces.

Taking its name from Fearnborginga, 'the village among the ferns on the hill', Farnborough developed because of its position on the London-Hastings road. The by-passing of the village in 1927 allowed Church Road, once the main coast road, to take on its now much more inviting peaceful aspect. Stage coaches used to make stops in the village — The Change of Horses and The George were both bustling coaching inns in the past.

The walk passes several 17th- and 18th-century cottages and begins in the churchyard of Farnborough Church. St Giles **A** was rebuilt in 1639, following a storm and the giant yew was planted outside the

west door at the same time. Look out for the gravestone of Levi Boswell, the gypsy chief who died in 1924 and his wife Urania (Gypsy Lee) beside the path.

THE HOME FARM

On emerging from the churchyard, moments after leaving buses, shops and houses, you are confronted with a view in which barely a house can be seen. A great field dotted with clumps of trees rolls down to a hidden road. Beyond rise the wooded slopes of the High Elms estate. Towards the end of the path where it reaches a little road, look out for the purple of wild mallow in the hedgerow. In spring the hedgerow is white with the flowers of hawthorn, once called 'quickset' by farmers, because of its ability to form an impenetrable hedge so quickly.

A few steps along a lane and over a wooded hill will bring you to High Elms Clock House **B**. This was once the Home Farm of the High Elms Estate and its tall, unusual, white-painted, wooden bell tower was added to the farmhouse in 1829. The bell was rung to indicate the starting and finishing of work. It remained in use for over 100 years when the Clock House was converted into a dairy. The High Elms estate itself was acquired in 1808 by John William Lubbock, a wealthy London

DEREK PRATT

▲ The church of St Giles was rebuilt in 1639 after a storm damaged it.

▲ *High Elms Clock House was a farm and dairy before it became a private country residence in the 19th century.*

banker, as a country residence. Produce from the farm was sent to the town house at St James' Place.

His grandson, who had the same name, was born in 1834 and was a distinguished scientist and social reformer. He had from an early age showed great interest in natural history and was encouraged in this study by his near neighbour Charles Darwin. He became president of the Linnaean Society. As an MP he was responsible for two pieces of legislation for which walkers will be grateful today — the Bank Holiday Act and the Preservation of Ancient Monuments Act.

The bridleway beside the Clock House leads up to a magnificent avenue of majestic beeches. The severe gales of 1987 flattened those on the east side of the slope and these have been replaced through the efforts of the Orpington Rotary Club, and two fellow Rotarian clubs from Europe.

THE COUNTRY VILLAGE

The route now passes through delightful Cuckoo Wood **C**, where beeches, maples and yew make a brilliant palette of colour in autumn. In spring the yellow archangel is spectacular (see Nature Guide: Flowers of the Wood) and other chalk-loving wild flowers are abundant in this area.

On leaving the wood, open fields are crossed to reach the lane into Downe **D**. Downe still remains a country village, with flint-faced cottages surrounding St Mary's Church. The church, also of local

THE WALK

FARNBOROUGH – DOWNE

The walk begins in the centre of Farnborough village at The George pub.

1 From The George in the centre of Farnborough Village, walk down Church Road and enter the churchyard of St Giles **A**. Continuing through the churchyard, pass through a gate into open country. Here, turn right along a field path and when, after about 200 yards (180 metres), it forks, keep left and continue across fields, slightly downhill to a road. Cross the road to North End Lane opposite and, just past North End Farm, take the right fork of the footpaths on the left. Going slightly uphill and ignoring all crossing paths, continue ahead through a wood and when this emerges on a golf course at the top, remain on the path, passing between a giant ash tree and an oak down to a road and High Elms Clock House **B**.

2 Cross the road to a bridlepath opposite and follow this uphill, across a golf course to reach a beechwood at the top. Continue ahead, through an avenue of magnificent beeches and, when this runs downhill to reach a wide crossing track, turn right. Follow the track, through woods **C** for 600 yards (550 metres). When the track bends sharply right beside a waymarker, turn

flint, dates from the 13th century and is similar in style to the Sussex downland churches, even to the extent of having a 'Sussex cap' spire upon its tower. The village has two excellent old pubs, The George and the 16th-century Queen's Head.

It is at Downe that you can decide whether to continue on the longer walk towards the house of Charles

Darwin; or the shorter version, which connects with it outside the village of Downe.

For those taking the longer walk, Downe is left by way of Luxted Road and in a short distance a turning is made beside the drained village pond along a footpath across fields to Down House **E**. It was here, for a period of 40 years, that

left downhill for a few paces to a stile on the right into a field. Cross the stile and, walking uphill with the wood now on the right, follow the field path for 100 yards (90 metres), and here, keeping left, cross the field, passing to the right of a pylon to a stile beside a spinney. Cross the stile and walk diagonally left across a meadow to a road. Turn left in this road and, when it reaches Mill Lane, keep left and follow the road into Downe **D** and St Mary's Church. Turn right into the churchyard and the centre of the village.

3 For the shorter walk, from the church, turn right down the village street, with the Queen's Head on your right, and, after 300 yards (270 metres), just beyond North End Lane, the route of the longer walk is regained. Continue ahead to three, weather-boarded cottages on the right, and follow the instructions from Stage 7. For the longer walk leave St Mary's Church, cross the road to Luxted Road and, after 120 yards (110 metres), turn left along a path (sign-posted Cudham) between two large houses. The path runs between flint walls into a field. Follow the yellow way-markers around the field to a stile.

4 Cross this stile turn immediately right and, following the hedgerow, continue to the end of the field to a swing gate. Go through the gate and cross the field, with

Down House **E** now in front, to a road.

5 Turn right past Downe House Cottage, and after 200 yards (180 metres) cross a stile on the right into a field. Keeping slightly right, cross the field to its far corner and pass through both a small gate and a second gate, painted green and, turning left over a stile, enter a field. Follow the path, running slightly right, across the field down to a wood. Cross the double-bar stile and continue down through the trees to a crossing path.

6 Here, turn right (sign-posted Holwood Farm) and follow this path along the top of a valley, with a golf course to your left. On reaching a road continue across to a path opposite and when the path ends at a crosspath, turn left, downhill through woodland. The path bends to the right and emerges once again above the valley golf course **F**. Follow this level path above the valley through fields and stiles for 3/4 mile (1.2 km). When the golf course ends in the valley below, enter a wood by a swing gate and, after 100 yards (90 metres), turn right at a signpost and walk uphill, crossing a stile. Continue uphill, across a wide ride, to a second stile into a field. Follow the broad path across the field to a road. Turn left in the road and continue ahead to three weather-boarded

cottages on your right.

7 Continue along this road for a further 150 yards (135 metres) and where this bends left, just past the coach-house of the Rookery, take the footpath on the right. Follow this path to a stile into a field and, keeping to the left, follow the field around to a gap in the hedge marked by a white post. Go through the gap and follow the white post markers to a lane. Cross the lane to a track opposite and, ignoring all paths to left and right, follow the lane for almost 1/4 mile (400 metres) to a crossing track. Go across the track to a stile in the hedge, and follow the clear path straight across the field, which slopes gently down to a road.

8 Cross the road to path opposite, and walk up the left side of the field beside a wood. At the top of the field, turn left along a path in this wood and past a marker **G** bearing the initials 'J.L.'. Here, turn right along a crossing path which continues through a partially cleared wood. When path emerges into a large field, continue straight ahead across this field, ignoring all crossing paths, and follow this path, with a wood now to your left and a view across the valley to the right. At the end of the wood, ignore a turn to the left, but continue ahead, beneath a white-painted bar along the path into Farnborough.

▶ *A walk through woods beyond Farnborough leads to Downe.*
The 16th-century pub, The Queen's Head, stands in the village that still retains its country atmosphere.

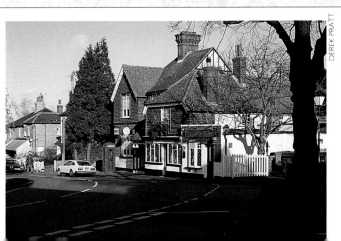

the great naturalist Charles Darwin lived and worked and where he wrote his *Origin of Species*. In this momentous work, he claimed that man was not created by God as had been recorded in the Book of Genesis, but had evolved very grad-ually over millions of years, an idea not unknown to science but one that caused a huge controversy in

DEREK PRATT

In 1842 Charles Darwin and wife Emma moved from London to the less hectic surroundings of Down House.

a footpath opposite a large Victorian house, The Rookery , and crossing several fields, you enter a delightful lane that provides nesting for many species of birds. Look out for the distinctive yellowhammers. This little lane ends at a hedge beyond which a field path descends to Shire Lane. The route continues across the little road and gently rises beside a wood, while to the right the soft contours of the field are broken by a number of copses.

A stone boundary marker with the initials 'J.L.' **G** reminds you that you are leaving John Lubbock's High Elms estate and the path, now running parallel to Shire Lane below, becomes a track, bounded by coppiced hazels and bearing the ancient name of Tye Lane. This name indicates that the village green is close by, as indeed it is, for Tye Lane brings you right into the middle of Farnborough.

the established church at the time.

The path takes you beside the garden of Down House and across the Sand Walk where Darwin daily strolled. It then descends to a path through woods, where the route follows a beautiful long valley, along remarkably even paths, some 400 feet (120 metres) above sea level **F**. Here the chalk downs provide an ideal habitat for violets, primroses and early purple orchids. Passing through several fields, which gently slope to the valley floor and golf course below, a beech wood is reached and another path across fields returns to the outskirts of Downe to connect with the shorter version of the walk.

After leaving the Downe Road by

The Origin of Species

After leaving school at the age of 16, Charles Darwin entered Edinburgh University with ambitions of a medical career. It soon became apparent to him that this was not where his interests lay and instead he found himself fascinated by the flora and fauna of the Scottish coast. In 1828, his medical career abandoned, he went to Cambridge, this time expecting to enter the Church. Again, his interests were those of a naturalist and, as at Edinburgh, he came into contact with scientific men who further stimulated his interest in the subject. While at Cambridge, an opportunity also arose to study geology and in 1831, through the suggestion of one of his university friends, he was invited to accompany the Admiralty survey ship HMS *Beagle* as a naturalist/ geologist on an expedition lasting five years, to South America and the Pacific.

It was from the observations, copious notes and the specimens he sent to England from the volcanic Galapagos Islands, situated 600 miles (960 km) off the coast of South America, that he later developed his theory of how life evolved. The importance of his

DOWN HOUSE

finds on the islands was not apparent to him at the time. He noted that the creatures of these islands, although having a marked relationship with each other and also with others in America, each differed slightly. His argument was: why should different inhabitants be created to perform the same functions in similar environments? He suggested that the differences were the result of natural

selection and the ability of species to adapt to their surroundings and climate. Of course, this conflicted fundamentally with the biblical explanation of the Creation.

Darwin developed these theories on his return to England and, in 1842, then married, bought Down House. It was here he wrote *The Origin of Species*, which was published in 1859, and where he lived for 40 years until his death in 1882.

The Admiralty survey ship, HMS Beagle, sailed to South America and the Pacific.

NATIONAL MARITIME MUSEUM, GREENWICH

HAMPSTEAD HEATH

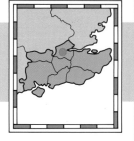

classical proportions of Kenwood House **F**. The walk then continues on its circular route through the Heath, taking in Parliament Hill **H** and Keats' House **J** before returning to the starting point.

Before the Industrial Revolution and the railways brought floods of immigrants to London from the rest of the country, Hampstead was a village on top of a hill, surrounded by fields, several miles to the north

◄ *The Vale of Health on Hampstead Heath was marshland until 1677. D.H. Lawrence and Edgar Wallace are among the writers that have lived nearby. The small copper (inset) is common on heaths and in urban gardens.*

From London's highest village around the wild spaces of the Heath

During the Middle Ages wolves roamed the wooded hills of Hampstead Heath. Today these wild canines have been replaced by their tamer relatives, domestic dogs, accompanied by thousands of their owners.

Covering more than 800 acres (324 hectares), Hampstead Heath in north London is a magnificent stretch of undeveloped countryside close to the heart of the city. Yet a hundred years ago it almost disappeared. Throughout the middle years of the last century the lord of the manor, Sir Thomas Marylon-Wilson, repeatedly tried to change the Heath's status from that of common land to private land that he could develop. He presented a series of private bills to Parliament that, if passed, would have enclosed the

Heath. Luckily, many of the local residents were influential people with the energy and power to thwart Marylon-Wilson's plans. His opponents formed the Heath Protection Committee which, over many years, effectively lobbied members of Parliament. By 1890 the Heath Protection Committee had succeeded in winning the battle and, except for the loss of many trees, the ancient Heath survived.

ELEGANT ARCHITECTURE

Starting at Hampstead underground station **A** this walk takes you from the cluster of elegant Georgian and Victorian streets that form London's highest urban village, Hampstead, across the Heath to the pleasing neo-

JOHN HESELTINE. INSET: M. J. GARWOOD/NHPA

FACT FILE

✳	Hampstead, north-west London
▭	Pathfinder 1159 (TQ 28/38), grid reference TQ 263857

miles 0 1 2 3 4 5 6 7 8 9 10 miles
kms 0 1 2 3 4 5 6 7 8 9 10 11 12 13 14 15 kms

◐	Allow 2½ hours; longer to visit Kenwood, Fenton or Keats' House
▬	Some of the paths are fairly steep and, because they are well-worn, can be very muddy during and after wet weather
P	At weekends, and on bank holidays, park in Hampstead village. On weekdays park in the car park on the edge of the heath, at the bottom of East Heath Road and walk a short distance to the beginning of the route
T	Hampstead underground station, on the Northern Line. Hampstead Heath British Rail station at South End Green (this will mean a short walk to the beginning of the route)
🏛 🍴	Pubs, shops and cafés in Hampstead village. Café at Kenwood House
WC	Kenwood House

35

of the capital. It first became popular in the early eighteenth century as a health resort. Those of London's citizens who wanted a break from the city's grimy streets headed for the cleaner air and iron-rich springs and wells of Hampstead. It is from this period of prosperity that some of the village's most beautiful buildings date. However, not all of Hampstead's visitors came in search of health and tranquillity. Many desired a livelier, holiday village, and alehouses, coffee shops, gambling dens and prostitutes were soon provided to cater for their tastes.

CONSTABLE'S GRAVE

One of Hampstead's most elegant streets from this period is Church Row ❸: the beautiful Georgian houses on the south side were built in the 1720s. The church of St John's is the parish church of Hampstead and was built in 1745. It has an ornate Renaissance-style ceiling that

was added in 1855. The beautiful wrought-iron gates to the churchyard were saved from the Duke of Chandos' country house, near Edgware in Middlesex, when it was demolished. Within the churchyard is the grave of John Constable, who painted many of his landscapes in

and around Hampstead village.

Opposite the church, the walk goes down Holly Walk, where refugees from the Terror of the French Revolution settled and built the Roman Catholic church of St Mary's in 1816. At the corner of Hollyberry Lane there is the first Hampstead police station. It was from here that, in the 1830s, the Hampstead Police Force set out to patrol the village's streets. At the end of Holly Walk, on the corner of Mount Vernon, stands Abernethy House, where the writer of *Treasure Island*, Robert Louis Stevenson, lived. From Mount Vernon the walk enters Holly Bush Hill.

It was at the Holly Bush pub, in 1829, that James Fenton inspired other Hampstead residents to take up the cudgels to preserve the Heath as common land open to all.

From Holly Bush Hill the walk soon enters Hampstead Grove. This has several fine houses, including

Romney House, a charming white weatherboard cottage built in 1797 for the artist George Romney. Another is New Grove House, which was inhabited by the nineteenth-century cartoonist and novelist George du Maurier.

The most beautiful house in

▼ *The Library at Kenwood House is a perfect example of Robert Adam's elegant interpretation of neoclassicism.*

◀ *The Orangery and Library at Kenwood House were added to the original building by Adam in 1764.*

Hampstead Grove, if not the whole of Hampstead, is Fenton House ❸, a William-and-Mary mansion of about 1693, with a pretty walled garden and a pair of superb wrought-iron gates. The house now belongs to the National Trust and is open to the public from March to October. The house contains the Benton-Fletcher collection of early keyboard instruments — a superb selection including a harpsichord that was played by Handel. There is also the Benning collection of porcelain and furniture donated with the house.

CITY VIEW

The walk continues along Admiral Walk (where John Galsworthy lived when he wrote his epic of middle-class life, *The Forsyte Saga*), into Windmill Hill and Judges Walk, to which London judges fled to escape the Great Plague in 1665. Shortly after Whitestone Pond the walk enters Hampstead Heath near the War Memorial that, at 442 feet (135 metres), marks London's highest point. From here there is a good view across the Heath and city.

HAMPSTEAD HEATH

The walk begins at Hampstead underground station at the corner of Heath Street and Hampstead High Street Ⓐ.

1▶ Turn left on coming out of the main entrance of the underground station, walk down Hampstead High St to the zebra crossing and cross over. Go through Oriel Place (opposite) and across Heath Street to Church Row Ⓑ. Walk along Church Row on the right-hand side and turn right into Holly Walk. Walk by the graveyard to the end of Holly Walk, then turn right into Mount Vernon.

2▶ At No 1 Mount Vernon cottages, turn right and immediately left into Holly Bush Hill. At the gates of Fenton House Ⓒ, bear right into Hampstead Grove. After Fenton House turn left into Admiral Walk. At the end of Admiral Walk, cross over Lower Terrace, going to the right of Fountain House, into the upper part of Windmill Hill.

3▶ Follow Windmill Hill up to Judges Walk. Turn right into Judges Walk, then left into Lower Terrace. Keep the new development on your left. At the top of Lower Terrace cross West Heath Road and walk down Whitestone Walk to North End Way. Cross

North End Way with great care and turn left. At the War Memorial in front of Heath House the road divides. Take the right-hand fork, Spaniards Way. About 55 yards (50 metres) along on the right a wide gravel path leads into the Heath.

4▶ Follow this path into the Heath, keeping the houses of the Vale of Health Ⓓ below and to the right. When the path divides, take the right fork and pass a small circular building on the right. Continue forward past the water fountain and toilets on the left.

5▶ Turn left over the bridge crossing a stream. Go straight ahead up the hill until you see a sign for Kenwood Woodland Area Ⓔ. Enter the Kenwood Woodland Area, taking the path to the left of the sign (ignore first left). When the path divides take the left fork that leads towards Kenwood House Ⓕ. At the lake turn left and cross the bridge. Cross the lawn and climb the steps to the left of the house. Turn right and walk past the front of the house.

6▶ After the house, take the left fork of the broad tarmac path through the gates, then turn right at the No Cycling sign. At the top of the hill cut across the Heath to the left and walk down to the tarmac path below. Follow

this path, keeping the first of Highgate Ponds Ⓖ on your right.

7▶ Turn right between the first and second ponds and follow the path, keeping the ponds on the left. After the third pond there is a sign saying Deep Water; take the asphalt path to the right and climb Parliament Hill Ⓗ. After the copse leave the path and walk left across to the top of Parliament Hill. Enjoy the panoramic view.

8▶ At the top of Parliament Hill turn right on the tarmac path. Walk past the houses on the left and carry on along the path. Take the path between the small ponds (Hampstead Ponds), then turn left and follow the path down to Heath Road.

9▶ At Heath Road, cross at zebra crossing, turn right and walk up South End Road past a parade of shops to Keats Grove on your left. Turn into Keats Grove. Pass Keats' House Ⓙ on your left. At the end of Keats Grove turn right into Downshire Hill; just after the pub and before the road joins Heath Road go left into Willow Road. Walk up Willow Road and take the right fork into Christchurch Hill. Continue walking up the hill into Well Walk Ⓚ.

10▶ Follow Well Walk until it forks, then take the right fork into Flask Walk. When you reach Hampstead High Street turn right to return to the undergound station or return to your car.

The wooded, sandy Heath has many varieties of trees and wild flowers and over 80 species of birds. The walk first passes alongside the Vale of Health Ⓓ which, until the 18th century, was an unhealthy swamp called Hatches Bottom. It was then drained, houses were built on it and the area was renamed.

From above the Vale of Health the walk heads towards Kenwood House Ⓕ, passing through the Kenwood Woodland Area Ⓔ. This wood, which was once part of the ancient and extensive Forest of Middlesex, gives an indication of how the Heath must originally have looked. The wood is now protected

as a Site of Special Scientific Interest and the path through it is fenced off from the trees that grow on either side to afford them protection.

In contrast to this unkempt woodland is the landscaped garden of Kenwood House. This includes a beautiful rose garden, some superb, mature beech trees, a sculpture by

▲ *Flask Walk, in Hampstead village, derives its name from the 18th century when water from the springs of Well Walk was bottled and sold here.*

Henry Moore and Dr Johnson's summerhouse. The gardens were laid out by the first Earl of Mansfield, who was George III's Lord Chief Justice. The house, with its stucco façade, was rebuilt for Mansfield, around its seventeenth-century original by Robert Adam in the 1760s. It was bequeathed to the nation in 1927 and contains a superb collection of paintings and furniture. It is open to the public daily.

From Kenwood the walk descends towards Highgate Ponds Ⓖ. These six ponds all have different

John Keats

One of the greatest Romantic poets of the 19th century lived in Hampstead, on the edge of the Heath. This was John Keats who shared a house with his friend and fellow poet, Charles Armitage Brown, from the summer of 1817 to September 1820, in what was then Wentworth Place and is now known as Keats Grove.

It was here that the passionate, red-haired poet wrote some of his most famous poems, including *Ode To A Nightingale* and *La Belle Dame Sans Merci*. It was Keats' most creative and productive period, probably because he had fallen in love with Fanny Brawne, who lived next door with her two sisters and their widowed mother.

Physically Keats was classically handsome with a lively expression. At school — perhaps to compensate for his short stature — he was aggressive and quarrelsome. But later on, at least towards his family and friends, he was loyal and caring. He nursed his frail brother Tom through several severe and demanding attacks of consumption.

When he, too, was fatally ill with the tuberculosis that had already killed his mother and brother, Keats

left Hampstead. Desperately in search of a cure, he sailed for Italy in 1820, but died in Rome the following year at the age of 25.

Keats' House, a small Regency house in Keats Grove, was the poet's home during an intensely creative period shortly before his death. It is open daily to the public.

characters and purposes. The first is the Stock Pond, the second the Ladies' Bathing Pond and the third a wildlife reserve. This fenced-off, neglected pond has a romantic, melancholy look. The next pond buzzes with the motors of model boats. The fifth is the Men's Bathing Pond and the final one is elegantly framed by willow trees. The two bathing ponds are open to swimmers throughout the year, whatever the weather.

GUNPOWDER PLOT

Close to the last two ponds is Parliament Hill Ⓗ, which at 319 feet (97 metres) gives a good view over London and usually provides plenty of breeze for the flying of kites. Its

◀ *The ponds on the Heath each serve a different purpose: two are for bathing, one for breeding fish, one for model boats and the others are for fishing.*

name comes from the Gunpowder Plot as it was here that Guy Fawkes and his fellow traitors met on 5th November 1605 in anticipation of watching the destruction of the Houses of Parliament.

On the other side of Parliament Hill are Hampstead Ponds, the source of the underground Fleet River that flows into the Thames. After Hampstead Ponds the walk leaves the Heath, going first to Keats' House in Keats Grove, then along Downshire Hill, where St John's Chapel still has box pews. Further on, Gainsborough Gardens is a circle of attractive Victorian villas around a garden. Next to Gainsborough Gardens is Well Walk Ⓚ; just to the right as you enter, a plaque on the wall of a house marks the site of the wells that made Hampstead popular 250 years ago. Further is Flask Walk, where the water was bottled for sale.

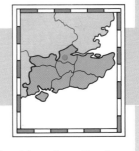
MICHAEL DENT. INSET: LAURIE CAMPBELL/NHPA

◄ *Water-lilies flourish on Stew Pond on Epsom Common. Such ponds always attract birdlife, especially the moorhen (inset) whose long toes allow it to walk on floating water plants.*

The successful 18th-century novelist Fanny Burney often visited Chessington Hall, close to the church in Garrison Lane. Her father, Dr Burney, wrote an epitaph to her host, Samuel Crisp, which is sited on the north wall of the church.

BURNT STUB MANOR

Chessington World of Adventures is a short distance from the town centre and is established in the grounds of a 17th-century house, Burnt Stub Manor. It is interesting to discover how the manor received such a name. The original manor was built in 1348 and became a school for archery. On her first visit

A walk through forests and farmland, close to central London

Chessington lies on the fringe of farmlands carved out of ancient oak woods. Only 12 miles (19 km) from central London, delightful, tree-shaded paths lead south, crossing fields and commons to enter part of the remaining forest. This walk follows some of these and explores the forest and its wildlife. The return route passes Horton Park Farm, where it is possible to see a wide range of farm animals in a working environment. There are many rare breeds including gentle, golden Guernsey goats, longhorn cattle and Icelandic sheep.

This is a full day's walk but an alternative would be to follow the first part of the walk only and combine this with a visit to Chessington World of Adventures, incorporating the Zoological Gardens.

Once in Surrey, and now within the Greater London boundary, Chessington Ⓐ is an ideal starting point for a variety of delightful country walks, well served by excellent bridleways and footpaths.

FACT FILE

- ☀ Chessington, 4 miles (8 km) south of Kingston

- ⌖ Pathfinder 1190 (TQ 06/16), grid reference TQ 179 633

  miles 0 1 2 3 4 5 6 7 8 9 10 miles
  kms 0 1 2 3 4 5 6 7 8 9 10 11 12 13 14 15 kms

- ◗ Allow a full day to explore the forest and visit Horton Park Farm. Chessington Adventure Park really requires three hours to get your money's worth

- ▬ Areas of long grass and muddy patches. Care needed as some road walking

- Ⓟ In front of Chessington South BR station or in the surrounding area — quiet side streets

- Ⓣ British Rail from Waterloo

- ⑂ Beside Chessington South BR station, at Chessington Adventure Park and at Horton Park Farm

- Ⓘ Chessington Adventure Park and Horton Park Farm

CHESSINGTON

A circular walk beginning from Chessington South Station.

1 From the station at Chessington **A**, turn right (station on your right) along Garrison Lane, over the railway bridge to the main road (A243). Cross the road and keep straight on down a lane signposted 'Bridleway for Claygate Common'. Keep to the lane, pass an entrance gate to the common on your left and Barwell Estate farm on your right. The lane bears left and becomes an attractive unmetalled path with views of fields and woods on your right. Pass beside a metal gate and a little further on you will see a large pond ahead of you on your right and a footpath sign on your left.

2 At the footpath sign do not follow the sign for Claygate Common, but turn left through an iron gate. Now you will see another sign pointing right for the Leatherhead Road (A243). Follow the direction of the sign down a narrow path winding through an oak wood. (The pond is still beyond the fields on your right.)

3 Leave the wood through a small wooden gate and walk on towards a small iron gate. Go through it and continue along the top of a field, with the high enclosure fence of Chessington Adventure Park close on your left.

4 When you reach the corner of the enclosure fence look left for a stile and a footpath sign for the Leatherhead Road. Turn left over the stile and keep straight on down the grassy path, past the exit for the

adventure park. The way is now gravelled for cars. When the exit track turns right, keep straight on over a wooden stile and along the grassy track ahead to cross a stile to Leatherhead Road (A243).

5 The entrance to Chessington World of Adventures **B** is on your left. To continue the walk, cross the Leatherhead Road and keep straight on following the sign marked 'Bridleway to Ashtead Common'. This leads through more oak woods, then bears right and becomes a gravel and cinder track. This leads to a barred metal gate, but a few paces to your left you will see a wooden stile that brings you to the B280 (Rushett Lane).

6 Cross the road and keep straight on over a field following the sign marked 'Bridleway to Ashtead Common', in the direction of the forest. Go through an iron gate and keep on to a footpath sign. Keep straight on in the direction marked 'Bridleway to Ashtead Common'. This brings you through an iron gate to a

footpath sign on the fringe of the forest **C**.

7 The walk goes to the left here, but it is well worth making a short detour to enjoy this ancient woodland. From the footpath sign walk straight ahead into the forest, following the direction marked 'Bridleway to Ashtead Station'. Follow this for just under ½ mile (800 metres) until a path joins from the left, the route of a Roman road. Retrace your steps to the signpost on the edge of the forest. Turn right,

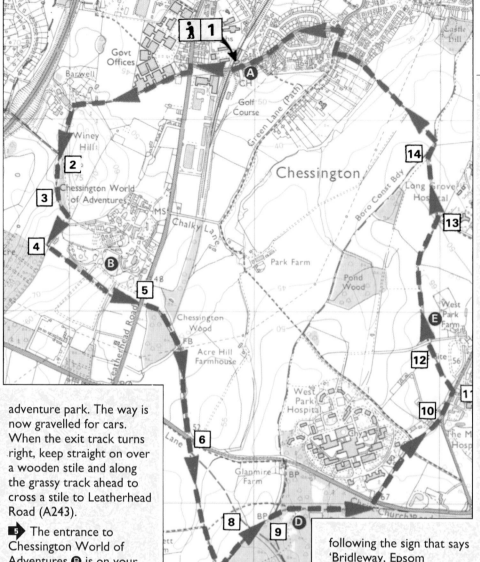

following the sign that says 'Bridleway, Epsom Common' (the forest is on your right).

8 Keep straight on over this crosstrack for Epsom Common.

9 The next crosstrack is not signposted. Keep straight on and follow the path as it leads to the smaller of two ponds on Epsom Common, Stew Pond **D** (the larger pond is a nature reserve). Pass the pond on the right and keep straight on along path through woods ahead. When the path divides, bear left for a short distance to the B280, here called Christ Church Road. Cross over road and walk straight ahead, following the bridleway sign for Horton Lane. Pass entrance to West Park Hospital on left, and continue down the access lane to Horton Lane.

10 Turn left and follow Horton Lane. Just past the entrance to the Manor Hospital, look carefully for a footpath sign on the left of the road.

11 Turn left, following the sign for Chessington. The way leads through long grass with a wooden fence close on your right.

12 After a short distance you come to a crosstrack and access to one of the parking areas for Horton Park Farm **E** on your right. Visit farm if you wish, then return to this point. Keep straight on over all crosstracks until you come to public footpath sign on right, in front of Long Grove Hospital.

13 Bear left here and keep on until you come to another crosstrack.

14 Navigate carefully here. Do not follow the main track, which keeps bearing a little to right, and do not turn left, but cross straight over and follow a narrow path that brings you to a wooden stile. Cross a stile into a field and bear right, then left around field to a stile on opposite side. Cross this stile and continue straight ahead. Go over the next stile and walk down to cross a small bridge over a stream. Keep straight on up a little path ahead, which brings you to a minor road. Turn right and follow the road to Garrison Lane, opposite the church of St Mary the Virgin. Turn left at the church and follow Garrison Lane back to the start of the walk.

ALL PHOTOS MICHAEL DENT

◄The agricultural buildings of Barwell Estate Farm feature in this area of fields, farmlands, commons and forest.

reducing it to a 'burnt stub'. Rebuilt in 1660 in the reign of Charles II, the lovely house visible today was aptly renamed.

Chessington Zoo was one of the first to allow animals, birds and reptiles as much freedom as was consistent with the safety of its visitors. It has now become part of a theme park — Chessington World of Adventures **B**.

CHILDREN'S ZOO

A variety of rides, a circus and the zoo provide entertainment and interest for all the family. The animals include many endangered species, among them gorillas, snow leopards and ruffed lemurs. Children have their own zoo where they can handle the animals.

Throughout this walk, the paths and lanes are shaded by magnificent oak trees. Here, part of the ancient oak forest **C** remains, a solid wall of

to the manor, Queen Elizabeth gave permission for archery to be practised on Sundays. During the Civil War it was a Royalist strong-hold. Cromwell's troops captured the house and razed it to the ground,

◄A narrow path winds through an oak wood. Oak trees predominate in this part of the country, remnants of ancient oak forests. The flat terrain (right) presents a more open view.

The Oak Tree

This massive, long-lived tree of the clay vales has earned a special place in the history of England. There are several varieties of oak but it is the pedunculate oak (*Quercus robur*), so-called because its acorns sprout from peduncles, or stalks, that has provided the strong wood for so many uses throughout English history from furniture to battleships — the famous 'hearts of oak' of Nelson's fleet.

Today, our oakwoods are even more precious. They provide the

The oak tree is useful to man for the hardness and durability of its timber and to wildlife as a host for many different species.

richest of all habitats for wildlife. Over 250 species of insect make their homes on oak and they attract birds such as treecreeper, nuthatch, pied flycatcher, wood warbler and jay. Young leaves are eaten by the caterpillars of many butterflies, including the lovely purple hairstreak. The crowns of the oak trees in the New Forest provide a haunt for the rare purple emperor butterfly.

Apart from providing food for wildlife, an abundance of acorns nourished the large herds of domestic pigs, once pastured in our forests, which were the mainstay of cottage economy. In the New Forest, this right of 'pannage' is still exercised.

Wild flowers flourish in the dappled light and shade and rich soil of our oakwoods. Bluebells, wood anemones, wood sorrel, primroses, wild garlic and, in the more open glades, foxgloves are abundant. Rarer species can be found here too, including wild Solomon's seal, several varieties of orchid and the wild gladiolus.

Oakwoods provide plentiful food and shelter for many of our shyest wild creatures, including fallow and roe deer, badgers and foxes. Even in decay, after an average life-span of around 250 years, an oak tree is valuable as host to mosses, lichens, ferns and fungi, helping to enrich the soil and thus support future generations of plant life.

▲ *St Mary the Virgin Church is in Chessington, a town with easy access to walks in the surrounding country.*

moorhens can be seen on the water.

Horton Park Farm **E** is a working farm, opened to the public in 1986, specializing in a wide range of domestic livestock, including many breeds that are virtually extinct. They form a fascinating link with past centuries and the country crafts that depended upon them.

COUNTRY CRAFTS

The primitive breeds of sheep on the farm often have coloured fleeces, prized by hand-spinners and weavers. Tuition is available in spinning and other aspects of working with fibres.

No artificial fertilizers are used and the fields are rich with a variety of grasses and flowering herbs. Tortoiseshell butterflies are attracted by the thistles left to grow on the edges of the fields.

green confronting the farmlands. Many of the older oaks have been pollarded — the tops have been removed for a variety of uses, resulting in the growth of many almost horizontal branches.

Leaving the forest, the walk now follows a bridleway that is crossed by the line of a Roman road and shortly reaches the Stew Pond **D**. In spite of its uninviting name ('stew' is an old word for a fishpond), this is a delightful small lake surrounded by woods. Wild ducks and

▶ *This oak forest is a forest in the true medieval sense, with open areas and commons on the sandier soils.*

heath. In 1497, it was the scene of King Henry VII's victory over Michael Joseph's Cornish rebels.

Next to the heath lies the Royal Park. It was enclosed in 1433 by Henry VI and later walled by James I. Its present design dates from 1662, when Charles II commissioned the French designer André Le Nôtre to produce plans for a formal layout of the site. Unfortunately, Le Nôtre never visited Greenwich and failed to take account of the steep escarpment dividing the park.

◀ *The gracious 17th-century buildings seen from the park include the Queen's House, designed by Inigo Jones, in the foreground with the twin cupolas of the Royal Naval College behind. The grey squirrel (inset) can be seen in the park.*

PHILLIP CRAVEN/ROBERT HARDING PICTURE LIBRARY. INSET: T & G COLEMAN/AQUILA

A London walk, rich in naval history and architectural interest

Greenwich is famous as the centre from which world time is measured. Lying on a bend in the River Thames 5 miles (8 km) downstream from the centre of London, it has a unique history. Settled by Romans, later used as a raiding base by Vikings, it was the birthplace of Henry VIII and a favoured residence of English monarchs for over two centuries.

The walk starts on the heath above Greenwich at the Neo-Gothic All Saints Church. In pre-Roman times paths ran down from the heath to the Thames below. The Romans built a road across the heath, connecting London with Dover and Canterbury.

HISTORY OF THE HEATH

Blackheath's proximity to London and commanding views made it strategically important. In 1011, the Viking army encamped there and later, both Wat Tyler's Peasant Army, in 1381, and Jack Cade's Rebels, in 1450, petitioned the King from the

---

FACT FILE

✳ Greenwich, 6 miles (9 km) east of Charing Cross

🗺 Pathfinder 1175 (TQ 27/37), grid reference TQ 395762

miles 0 1 2 3 4 5 6 7 8 9 10 miles
kms 0 1 2 3 4 5 6 7 8 9 10 11 12 13 14 15 kms

◔ Allow 4 hours including visits to historic sites

▬ Easy, level paths

P In Blackheath and Greenwich Park. Very little parking in Greenwich itself at weekends

T BR stations in Blackheath, Greenwich, Maze Hill. Boat service: see Greenwich Pier for times and destinations. Regular bus service (53) into Central London

🍴 Numerous cafés and pubs on the route of the walk

WC Next to main top gates, at the Old Royal Observatory and next to the Cutty Sark

🏰 Old Royal Observatory, National Maritime Museum, The Queen's House, *Cutty Sark*; admission charge for all. Day passport and family ticket

THE WALK

BLACKHEATH – GREENWICH PARK – GREENWICH

The walk begins at the main (north) entrance to All Saints Church, All Saints Drive, Blackheath.

1 Walk north across the heath towards Greenwich Park Gate Lodge, which is visible from the church. (Use Canary Wharf Tower as a marker — the point of the Tower rises above the main Shooters Hill Road by the pelican crossing.) Enter park through main gates.

2 Follow the avenue straight ahead. After 400 yards (360 metres) the road swings left. Carry straight on to the statue of General Wolfe and the viewing area **A**.

3 Left of the statue is the Old Royal Observatory **B**. Follow the path alongside the Observatory through the iron kissing gate. Cross the East-West Longitude line and continue down to the road. Turn right and follow the railings downhill. After 150 yards (135 metres) follow the railings round to the right away from the road. Continue diagonally right across the park. After 140 yards (126 metres) the path narrows. Continue for another 250 yards (225 metres) and leave the park by the pedestrian gates next to the Maritime Museum **C**.

4 Enter the grounds of the Maritime Museum through gates on the immediate left. Turn left and follow the path past the entrance to the Museum. Continue for 200 yards (180 metres) then re-enter the park by the gate on the left opposite the museum café. Turn right and follow the path to the main bottom gates. Leave park and take the first turning on the left (Nevada Street). At the end of Nevada Street, turn right and follow the road round into Greenwich High Road. St Alphege Church **D** is on the left. Cross at the zebra crossing to the railings of the church.

5 Bear right and continue for a few paces, then cross at the zebra crossing where Creek Road intersects on the left and carry on straight ahead. The Tourist Information Centre is across the road on the right-hand side. Continue on to the pedestrian concourse where the *Cutty Sark* **E** and the *Gypsy Moth IV* are in dry dock.

6 Take the path that runs alongside Greenwich Pier with the Thames on the left. Continue past the Naval College **F** to the Trafalgar Tavern **G** on Park Row. Take the alley that runs behind the Trafalgar Tavern and past the front of the Yacht Tavern to St Trinity Hospital **H** and Greenwich Power Station.

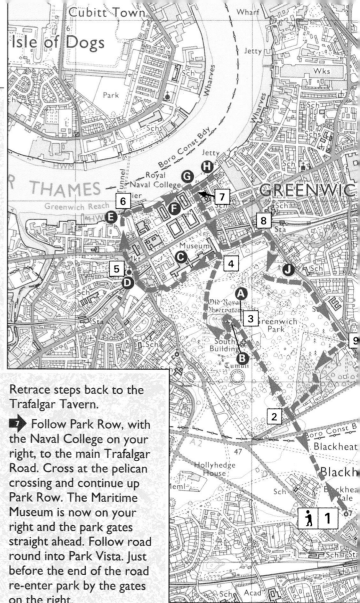

Retrace steps back to the Trafalgar Tavern.

7 Follow Park Row, with the Naval College on your right, to the main Trafalgar Road. Cross at the pelican crossing and continue up Park Row. The Maritime Museum is now on your right and the park gates straight ahead. Follow road round into Park Vista. Just before the end of the road re-enter park by the gates on the right.

8 Take the left-hand path until the corner, then cut right across the grass to a flight of steps. Climb steps and continue to the top of the hill where three paths meet. Take the left-hand path, ignoring the right-hand path that runs down a steep hill. Ahead and to the left is Vanbrugh Castle **J**. Continue until a number of paths meet. Follow the path to the right running alongside the park wall for 400 yards (360 metres).

Where the path turns sharp right, enter the Flower Gardens by the gate ahead on the right.

9 Follow the path ahead for 250 yards (225 metres). In front of the pond take the left-hand path and continue round the garden to the gate. Leave the gardens and turn left for the main top entrance to the park. Return to All Saints Church across the heath.

Instead of the central tree-lined avenue leading up to the Queen's House, it actually leads to the edge of a 100-foot (30.5-metre) drop.

This oversight, however, provides the modern visitor with unparalleled views over London. From the viewing area **A**, St Paul's Cathedral, the Docklands developments and the great sweep of the River Thames through London are all visible.

The Old Royal Observatory **B** next to the viewing area was commissioned by Charles II and designed by Christopher Wren. Built in 1675, on the site of an old Watch Tower, there have been a number of additions to Wren's original design.

The Observatory later moved to Sussex and is now in Cambridge. The Greenwich buildings these days house an exhibition of scientific instruments and a planetarium. On one wall of the Observatory is the GMT 24-hour clock and nearby a line on the path showing the Greenwich Meridian. There cannot

▲ *The statue of General Wolfe beside the Old Royal Observatory, built in 1675 and designed by Christopher Wren.*

be many walks in this country that allow you to stand with a foot in each hemisphere.

In 1894 there was an attempt to blow up the Observatory — but the bomb exploded prematurely, killing the carrier. It was this incident that inspired Joseph Conrad's classic story, *The Secret Agent*.

THE QUEEN'S HOUSE

The Maritime Museum **C** contains the finest collection of naval artefacts in the country. At the centre of the museum is the Queen's House. It was built as a gift from James I to his wife, Queen Anne, although it was not completed until the reign of Charles I. Designed by Inigo Jones, it is one of the finest examples of his work, drawing heavily on the Italian Villa style with simple lines and little outward decoration.

The work of another great English architect is well represented in Greenwich. Nicholas Hawksmoor was commissioned to provide a new parish church after a great storm in 1710 destroyed the old one. He built St Alphege **D** on the supposed site of the martyrdom of Archbishop

Alphege by the Danes in 1012. The many famous people who have attended the church have their names recorded on plaques and tombstones. Across from the church is the covered market, which holds a Craft Fair at weekends.

TEA CLIPPER

The *Cutty Sark* **E** is perhaps Greenwich's best known landmark. The last surviving clipper ship, she sits in dry dock overlooking the Thames. Built in 1869 on the Clyde, the *Cutty Sark* could reach a speed of over 17 knots and cover 360 miles (576 km) a day. Originally built for the tea trade, she made her name as a wool clipper sailing back and

forth to Australia. Alongside the *Cutty Sark* lies *Gypsy Moth IV* sailed by Sir Francis Chichester. Although dwarfed by its famous neighbour, the *Gypsy Moth* was in fact the largest single-handed yacht ever built when it was completed in 1966.

RIVERSIDE SITE

Just downstream is the Royal Naval College **F**. The site it occupies is one of the most historic locations in Greenwich: the original foundations of the Royal Palace of Placentia. The Palace was used by the English Monarchy from 1447 until the Restoration. It fell into disrepair during the interregnum and was pulled down by Charles II. The King

had grand plans for the riverside site, but his grandiose designs were never realized. A notoriously fickle monarch, Charles lost interest in the project and only the King Charles building was completed.

It was not until the reign of William and Mary — who granted a charter for the foundation of a Royal Hospital for Seamen in 1694 — that work re-started on the site, this time under the direction of Sir Christopher Wren. From the outset, however, great restrictions were placed on his design. Queen Mary insisted he maintain a line of sight from the Queen's House to the Thames. Wren was left with little choice but to create an avenue

◄ *A detail of the architectural elegance of the Queen's House. The design by Inigo Jones was his first major work and was based on the principles of the Italian architect Palladio.*

▼ *A three-masted tea-clipper, the* Cutty Sark *was famous in its day as the fastest ship of its type. Launched in 1869, it was berthed in Greenwich in 1957.*

Henry VIII in Greenwich

During the reign of Henry VIII (1509-1547) Greenwich enjoyed its heyday as a Royal residence. Henry was born and grew up in the Palace of Placentia on the banks of the River Thames. When he became king his court was often in residence at Greenwich.

Henry would hawk and hunt in the Royal Park and inspect his ships on the Thames. His passion for shipbuilding led him to establish new shipyards nearby. He also built an armoury at Greenwich, bringing in German craftsmen to create fine suits of armour.

Henry's court was more European in style than anything England had seen before. There were masques, dances and banquets often attended by hundreds of guests. Henry was a keen sportsman and Greenwich Park witnessed numerous jousts and tournaments, many of which Henry competed in himself. One of the most splendid occasions must have been the reception given to Emperor Charles V who arrived at Greenwich in a procession of 30 barges, bringing with him a retinue of 2,000.

Despite the pageantry, Greenwich was also the scene of some of Henry's darker moods. The arrest of Anne Boleyn's brother and friends was at a tournament in Greenwich Park. Later, King Henry signed her death warrant at the Palace of Placentia and she was beheaded on 19th May 1536.

Greenwich Palace from the Thames, the birthplace of Henry VIII in 1491. The site is now the Royal Naval College

▲*The Queen's House flanked by the Royal Naval College. Designed by Wren, the college was commissioned by William and Mary as a naval hospital.*

through the middle of his building. This effectively made the Queen's House the centrepiece of his design, a role the building is simply not grand enough to fulfil.

Next to the Naval College is the Trafalgar Tavern **G** on Park Row. It was built in 1837 and became famous for its Cabinet Whitebait Dinners when members of the Government would come down the Thames in barges to dine there. The pub is mentioned in Charles Dickens' *Our Mutual Friend* and the author was a regular visitor.

Down the alleyway behind the Trafalgar is Trinity Hospital **H**. It was established in 1613 by the Earl of Norfolk who founded a number of such charitable institutions. Today it still fulfils its original purpose of providing homes for the elderly. Next to the hospital is the massive Greenwich Power Station, built in 1906 to provide London's then-growing tram network with electricity. These days it is used as a back-up power supply for the London Underground.

VANBRUGH CASTLE

The path leading to Vanbrugh Castle **J** has excellent views back over the Power Station and across the Thames to the East End of London. Vanbrugh Castle lies just outside the walls of the park. Sir John Vanbrugh designed the building and lived there between 1717 and 1726. The castle was known as 'The Bastille' both because of its appearance — resembling a medieval fortress — and because its architect had been held in the French prison as an English spy.

▶*Trafalgar Tavern, on the Thames, dates from 1837 and was visited regularly by Charles Dickens.*

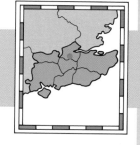

11

HILLS OF CROYDON

An unexpectedly rural walk in the heart of a London suburb

The London Borough of Croydon, which has grown enormously this century with the overspill population from the metropolis, may seem an unlikely spot for a rural ramble. The route passes through green surroundings for well over half its distance, and most of the remainder is on footpaths through residential areas.

The circular route takes in some very attractive woodland and parkland scenery, a splendid ridge walk, a nature reserve and a beautiful landscaped garden.

VIEWS OVER LONDON

The walk begins at South Croydon Station, in the heart of a residential area. However, suburban development soon gives way to the woodland of Croham Hurst. The spine of the woods is the whaleback hump of Breakneck Hill **A**, the site of a prehistoric settlement. The path

MARK CRICK. INSET: VIC COBBOLD/SWIFT PICTURE LIBRARY

▲*Coombe Wood, below Addington Hills, has lovely, landscaped gardens. The edible oyster mushroom (inset) can be found from autumn to spring on both living trees and fallen timber.*

goes along the crest of its ridge, which rises to 472 feet (144m) and offers views in several directions.

On the other side of Littleheath Woods **B** is Bramley Bank Nature Reserve **C**, run by the London Wildlife Trust. It has five species of amphibians and interesting flowers.

Addington Hills **D** are a haven of woodland and rough grassland. On a clear day, there is a panorama right

across London, to the Chilterns in the west and Epping Forest in the east. Major landmarks are clearly identified on a viewing platform.

The route descends into Coombe Wood **E**, where there is a fine landscaped garden and a cafeteria where the Chinese proprietors calculate your bill on an abacus.

Finally, the walk follows the Vanguard Way, a long-distance path, through Lloyd Park **F**, before heading back to South Croydon. Lloyd Park was once farmland but, in 1927, was presented to Croydon Corporation in memory of the landowner, Frank Lloyd.

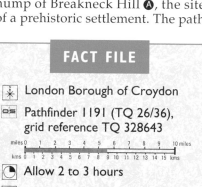

FACT FILE

* London Borough of Croydon

* Pathfinder 1191 (TQ 26/36), grid reference TQ 328643

miles 0 1 2 3 4 5 6 7 8 9 10 miles
kms 0 1 2 3 4 5 6 7 8 9 10 11 12 13 14 15 kms

* Allow 2 to 3 hours

* Mostly woods and parkland, with some steep hills

* **P** Car park at South Croydon BR station

* **T** Frequent trains from London to East Croydon and South Croydon stations. Good bus service

* Pubs in South Croydon, tea rooms at Addington Hills and Coombe Wood

* **WC** Toilets at Addington Hills and Coombe Wood

THE WALK

CROYDON

The walk begins at South Croydon BR station.

1 Turn left beside the forecourt and descend the long flight of steps to the road. Turn left. In 150 yards (140m) cross and turn right up Moreton Road. Pass Doveton Road to bear left; then, where Moreton Road bears right under the bridge, go left up the steps and keep ahead to cross a footbridge over the disused railway line. Follow the path, bearing right onto the road, then pass a school and bear left to the major road. Cross, then follow the footpath ahead, until you reach Croham Manor Road.

2 Cross to the grassy area at the entrance to Croham Hurst. Turn right by the bench seat, and enter a wood on a wide path rising gently. After 100 yards (90m), bear left up a steep gravel path to reach the open, grassy ridge of Breakneck Hill **A**. Follow the ridge for 700 yards (630m); about halfway along divert to the right on the spur for a better view, then return to the main path. At the end of the ridge, descend steeply, bearing right to join the road.

3 Cross and turn left along the pavement for 400 yards (360m), then cross back over and turn left along Queenhill Road, crossing a major road and a T-junction, and going ahead up some steps into Littleheath Woods **B**.

4 Keep ahead on a narrow path for 80 yards (75m), then turn left along a wider path to an open, grassy area. Turn right along the edge of an open

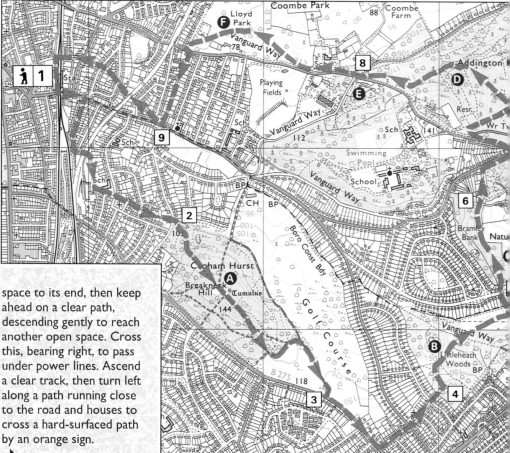

space to its end, then keep ahead on a clear path, descending gently to reach another open space. Cross this, bearing right, to pass under power lines. Ascend a clear track, then turn left along a path running close to the road and houses to cross a hard-surfaced path by an orange sign.

5 Go half-right across the grass to a fence, beneath a sign 'London Wildlife Trust : Bramley Bank Nature Reserve' **C**. Take the left-hand entrance and follow the main path ahead. Fork right to follow a series of short, white-topped posts. At the end of the bank, descend to the corner of a field fence. Keep ahead beside the fence, to the road, where there is a reserve information board.

6 Follow the road ahead to the T-junction. Turn right to the main road, then turn left to cross it on a zebra crossing and follow the dirt track beside it. Cross a minor road and turn right on a path through woods. After 50 yards (45m) turn right on the major track to the car park and driveway at the

main entrance to Addington Hills **D**.

7 Turn left along the driveway past a Chinese restaurant to the viewing platform. Go down a steep gully to the left of the platform, turn right at the bottom, then left. Go straight ahead to the T-junction of paths just 20 yards (18m) from the road and turn right. Follow the path to the car park by the junction of Oaks Road and Coombe Lane. Almost opposite is the entrance to Coombe Wood **E**.

8 Go along the right-hand pavement of Coombe Road to a large open space (Lloyd Park **F**). Follow a grassy path half-right away from the road for some distance, then bear left to a

children's playground beside a bomb crater. Keep ahead in the same direction, to the right of a large brick pavilion, then between the tennis courts and the bowling green to Lloyd Park Avenue. Turn left to the main road. Cross it and turn left then immediately right up a bridleway, to a road.

9 Turn right, then right again into Campden Road, and almost immediately left along a footpath. Follow the footpath across a road, then over a footbridge (across a disused railway line) and another three roads, to reach the bridge over the main railway line. Cross and turn sharp left through a gap in the wall, to follow the footpath back to the station.

COMMON INTERESTS

12

GREATER LONDON

Tracing the history of a leafy common in London's suburbia

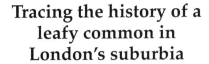

▲ *A local landmark, the 19th-century windmill now houses a museum and tea-room. Bogbean (above right) grows in pools and wet areas on the common.*

There is evidence of man using Wimbledon Common since Neolithic times, when its numerous springs and commanding views made it an ideal location for a settlement. Today, it is a perfect spot for those seeking to escape the noise and traffic of the capital.

The walk begins in the south-east corner of the common, not far from Cannizaro House and Park **Ⓐ**. The house is now a hotel and restaurant, but the park is open to the public all year round. The first reference to the house is in 1727, when it was owned by Thomas Walker, commissioner of customs to King George I.

FAMOUS CONNECTIONS

Since then, it has had a string of wealthy owners and played host to many famous people. Towards the end of the 19th century, the owner, Mrs Schuster, entertained lavishly and her garden parties attracted, among others, the Prince and Princess of Wales, Lord Tennyson, Oscar Wilde and Henry James. The house was named after the Duke of

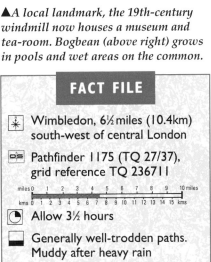

FACT FILE

⁎ Wimbledon, 6½ miles (10.4km) south-west of central London

▨ Pathfinder 1175 (TQ 27/37), grid reference TQ 236711

miles 0 1 2 3 4 5 6 7 8 9 10 miles
kms 0 1 2 3 4 5 6 7 8 9 10 11 12 13 14 15 kms

◷ Allow 3½ hours

▬ Generally well-trodden paths. Muddy after heavy rain

Ⓟ Car parks and off-road parking in Wimbledon village and around the common

Ⓣ London Underground District Line and BR trains from Waterloo to Wimbledon

▤ Many pubs, cafés and restaurants in Wimbledon. Windmill Museum Tea Rooms open daily

wc Windmill Museum

I Windmill Museum open April-October, weekends and Bank Holidays, 2-5pm

Cannizaro, an impoverished Sicilian who married a wealthy English-woman and moved there in 1817.

Just beyond the clubhouse of the Royal Wimbledon Golf Course is Caesar's Camp **Ⓑ**, now barely discernible, which provides the earliest evidence of settlement in Wimbledon. The site has no known connection with Roman Britain, and has been known by this name only since the last century. It is an Iron Age hill fort of a type found extensively in southern England.

Caesar's Well **Ⓒ**, across the common, has no connection with the Romans either. The well is now filled in, but there is still an outlet for the spring, which flowed even during the drought of 1976 when the rest of the Common was tinder dry.

From the well, the path runs beside the Queen's Butt **Ⓓ**. This raised mound is the remains of a firing range used by the National Rifle Association, who held annual competitions on the common between 1860 and 1889. On the opening day of their first meeting, Prince Albert and the Royal entourage watched as Queen Victoria fired the first shot of the tournament. A special mechanical rest was constructed for her rifle so that all she had to do was pull a silken cord to fire. Not surprisingly, she scored a bullseye. A little further on is the KRR Stone. This commemorates the King's Royal Rifle Corps, who were encamped on the

THE WALK

WIMBLEDON COMMON

The walk begins by the war memorial at the junction of Parkside and The Causeway.

1 Cross the common towards Rushmere Pond. Take the path round the left-hand side of the pond and continue across Cannizaro Road towards the pink house on the edge of the Common.

2 Facing Cannizaro House and Park **A** turn right along West Side. Continue over The Causeway to West Place. Bear left along North View, then continue ahead across the common to a gate marked 'Access only'.

3 Turn right along the track. After 200 yards (180m), at a gate marked 'Access to Warren Farm', take the narrow, fenced path ahead and slightly to your left through Caesar's Camp **B**. The path bears left. After another 200 yards (180m) it meets a crossing path.

4 Continue straight ahead for 300 yards (270m). Just before a bridge, turn right to follow Beverley Brook. At a bridge by Brook Cottage, take the path ahead and to your right, ignoring a path running sharp right.

5 Shortly before the trees clear at the brow of the hill, take a narrow path to your right to Caesar's Well **C**, which is surrounded by tall Scots pines. Retrace your steps to the main path and turn right. At the top of the hill, fork left. Continue for 300 yards (270m), past the Queen's Butt **D**.

6 Just before the KRR Stone, go left on a crossing path. After 300 yards (270m), follow the path round to the right. After another 300 yards (270m), in front of a line of trees, the path divides in several directions. Take the path going ahead and slightly left, and follow it down to Queen's Mere.

7 At the lake, turn right along its edge. Ignore a path to your right, then take an uphill path to your right beside a small stream. At the top of the hill, turn left and follow the path round to the right to the entrance to the Windmill Museum **E**.

8 Follow the hedge round to your right, then go straight ahead on a wide, sandy path alongside a bridleway. Continue for 100 yards (90m), then take the first path on the left of the bridleway. Follow this path back to the start.

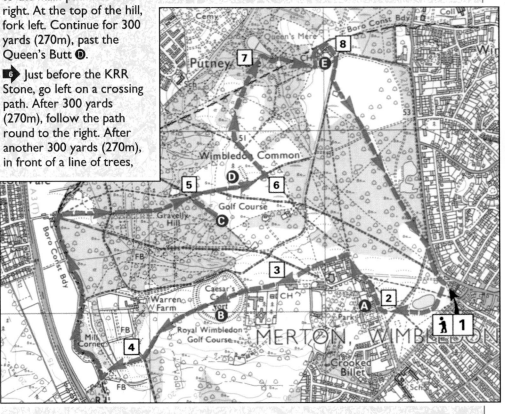

▼ *Caesar's Well is a natural spring which was once used as a well.*

Common before being posted overseas during World War I.

The windmill **E**, overlooking Putney Vale, was built in 1817 by Charles March, a Roehampton carpenter. The original mill had a shorter tower and was built entirely of timber above the ground floor level. A chute delivered sacks of flour from the first floor into waiting carts. The mill ceased working in 1860, and five years later the lower part of the building was converted into cottages.

In the 19th century, Thomas Hunt Dann worked at the mill, and lived with his wife and son at a nearby cottage. He was also the constable of the common, charged with ensuring that law and order prevailed. This was never an easy task, as, in those days, the common was a popular spot for duelling.

The practice continued as a means of settling disputes long after it had been outlawed. On 12 September 1840, a famous duel took place on the Common when Lord Cardigan wounded a Captain Tuckett. Thomas Dann arrested Cardigan, who stood trial in the House of Lords but was acquitted.

From the mill, the route follows a bridleway, then branches off across the common, eventually leading back to the war memorial.

A RIGHT ROYAL PARK

13

A haven of tranquillity within sight of the City of London

Richmond Park is the largest of the Royal Parks, covering an area of around 2,500 acres (1,000ha). Its bracken-covered, rolling grassland landscape, dotted with plantations, supports a diverse flora and fauna, including ancient oaks, herds of deer, and many species of birds. The park was declared a Site of Special Scientific Interest in 1992. It provides a peaceful, natural setting for a country walk, yet on a clear day there are excellent panoramas of Central London.

ROYAL FAVOURITE

The walk begins at Pembroke Lodge **A**, an attractive building set in pleasant gardens. 'Molecatcher's Cottage' originally occupied the site, but Elizabeth, Countess of Pembroke, one of the reigning beauties in George III's court, had the place rebuilt and renamed. The King visited her there on occasions.

In 1847, Queen Victoria granted

FACT FILE

✳	Richmond Park
🗺	Pathfinders 1174 (TQ 07/17) and 1175 (TQ 27/37), grid reference TQ 187729

miles 0 1 2 3 4 5 6 7 8 9 10 miles
kms 0 1 2 3 4 5 6 7 8 9 10 11 12 13 14 15 kms

🕐	Allow 3 hours
▭	Mostly level walking on dry, well-marked footpaths
P	Pembroke Lodge car park at the start
T	BR from Waterloo and London Underground District Line trains to Richmond. For bus service information, Tel. (071) 222 1234
🍺	None on the route. Many pubs in Richmond
🍴	Pembroke Lodge cafeteria
WC	Pembroke Lodge
🏰	Richmond Park is closed to vehicles between dusk and dawn; closing times are posted on the gates

the tenancy of Pembroke Lodge to Lord John, the first Earl Russell. His grandson, the philosopher, mathematician and social reformer Bertrand Russell, lived here as a child, from 1876 to 1890.

Beyond Pembroke Lodge Gardens, the route continues through open parkland, along a ridge topped

◄ *The rhododendrons and azaleas in Isabella Plantation produce a stunning display in late spring. Red deer stags (below) can be seen and heard rutting from late August to early October.*

by an avenue of hornbeams, towards Ham. Along the way there are fine views over Petersham Park, Ham Bottom and beyond.

MARTIN'S OAK

The 'yaffle' call of the green woodpecker is often heard here, and there are many ancient oaks, including a magnificent specimen known as Martin's Oak **B**. The Victorian painter, John Martin, reputedly enjoyed quietly sketching the views — a far cry from the vast depictions of apocalyptic catastrophe for which 'Mad Martin' later became famous — while seated at a bench that formerly circled the mighty trunk.

A little further on, to your right,

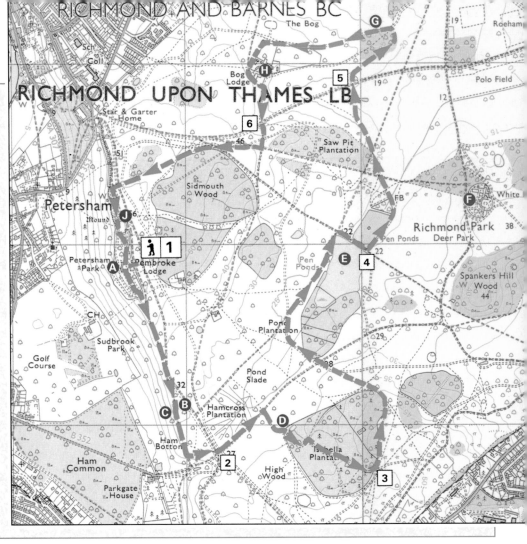

THE WALK

PEMBROKE LODGE – ISABELLA PLANTATION – BOG LODGE

The walk begins at the Pembroke Lodge car park.

▶ Enter the grounds of Pembroke Lodge **A**, and turn left on the path in front of the house to walk through the garden. Follow a gravel path through rhododendrons and exit via a gate in the deer fence. Go directly ahead, along the top of a ridge. At the end of an avenue of hornbeams, the gravel path runs very close to the road for about 50 paces. Take a level, grassy path which forks right, through the bracken. About 50 yards (45m) along this path, you pass a large old oak **B** on your left, then a mound **C**

is a large mound **C** topped by a gaunt oak. The mound, best seen in winter or spring before the bracken has grown tall, is believed to be a prehistoric tomb. Other evidence of prehistoric occupation of the area includes worked flints found in the gravel of Pen Ponds.

WOODLAND GARDEN

On the way from Ham Cross, you may well spot deer in Hamcross Plantation, to your left. It is a favoured spot for them, particularly in late spring, when the streams and ditches in the wood afford some protection for the new-born fawns.

The Isabella Plantation **D** was originally enclosed by Viscount Sidmouth, Deputy Ranger of the park, in the 19th century. The area was named 'Isabell Slade' as early as 1771, but no record has yet been discovered associating a lady of that name with the park. In recent years, a delightful woodland garden has been created, with a wide collection of acid-loving, flowering shrubs such as rhododendron, azalea, camellia, magnolia and heather. Through the centre runs a lovely brook, artificially diverted and edged with waterside plants.

BIRD SANCTUARY

From here, the route winds north past Pond Plantation. This bird sanctuary is closed to the public, but as you skirt the edge in May or June its delicate silver birches and colourful rhododendrons make a

spectacular show, especially when reflected in Upper Pen Pond.

Created in the 18th century from old gravel pits, Pen Ponds **E** now attract many visitors, as well as large numbers of waterfowl: mallard, tufted duck, pochard, teal, gadwall, wigeon, shoveler, golden-eye, gulls, herons and Canada geese visit regularly, and, more rarely, there are goosanders, red-necked

◀ *The former home of a royal favourite, Pembroke Lodge is today a pleasant place to take tea. Majestic trees such as Martin's Oak (right) may be as old as the park itself. John Martin's portrait of this tree hangs in the V & A Museum.*

BOTH PHOTOS: SUE MORRIS

on your right. When the path starts to dip, turn left by a hollow tree stump, up to the road at Ham Cross.

2 Carefully cross the road and the horse ride, and follow a tarmac road ahead. Turn right along a gravel drive to enter the Isabella Plantation **D**. Inside, a main gravel path leads ahead, but there are many side paths worth exploring; head in a general uphill direction to reach the gate on the opposite (south-east) side.

3 Leave the plantation and follow a path left alongside the fence. At the northern tip of the plantation, the path divides into three; take the middle path, with the corner of Pond Plantation directly ahead. Cross the tarmac road and follow the path round to your right along the horse ride. At a junction with a wide, gravel path, turn right along it towards Pen Ponds **E**. At the far end of Upper Pond, turn right and walk to the far side of Lower Pond.

4 Turn left along Lower Pond. At its end, continue ahead. Cross a footbridge and continue towards the trees of Saw Pit Plantation. Cross the wide avenue of Queen's Ride, with White Lodge **F** away to your right. Continue to walk ahead, skirting the plantation on your left. As the path veers away from the trees and descends to the road, keep just to the left of a small pond.

5 Cross the road and bear right to skirt Barn Wood. Continue uphill, with the trees on your left, until you reach a junction of two paths by some ancient oaks and newly planted saplings **G**. Turn left and continue along the edge of the woods until you see a fenced field enclosure ahead. Take the right-hand path, between this fence and the horse ride (beware of rabbit-holes), heading towards a distant church spire. By a gnarled stump, turn left along the fence, skirting the buildings of Bog Lodge **H**. At the tarmac drive to the lodge's main entrance, turn right to the main road.

6 Cross the road and continue ahead up a gravel path. Cross Queen's Ride, then take the well-worn path right, towards Sidmouth Wood. Continue with the trees to your left. At the corner of the plantation, take the wide grassy path to your right, and make for a small brick building in the distance. Cross the horse ride and road to the north entrance to Pembroke Lodge Gardens. Take the main path ahead. After the laburnum walk, fork left to King Henry VIII's Mound **J**. Descend the mound on the other side, and rejoin the main path to return to the start of the walk.

grebes and migrating terns.

The route crosses Queen's Ride, a fine avenue bordered by oaks and sweet chestnuts. It is named after George II's Queen Caroline. The Classical building visible at the end of the ride is White Lodge **F**, built in about 1728 by George II as a retreat for himself and his family.

Viscount Sidmouth lived there from 1801 to 1844, and was visited by many eminent men, including Sir Walter Scott (who set part of his

BOTH PHOTOS: SUE MORRIS

▲ *A pleasant prospect from Ham Cross. Pen Ponds (left) attract many birds, including one or two pairs of mute swans that regularly breed.*

novel *Heart of Midlothian* in the park), R B Sheridan and Admiral Lord Nelson. In September 1805, five weeks before Trafalgar, Nelson is said to have sketched his battle plan in wine on the dining table. Since 1954, White Lodge has been occupied by the Royal Ballet School, and can be visited by the public

only on occasional open days.

Rounding Saw Pit Plantation — the park's natural resources have always been exploited — the path leads to Barn Wood, which contains some of the finest old oaks in the park. Deanes Lane, an ancient drovers' road, ran through the wood on its way from Kingston to Mortlake, and some of the oldest trees lean in from a bank that marks the line of the lane.

Close by the older generation of oaks, new saplings, protected from the deer by wooden fences, mark the new Two Storm Wood ⓖ, planted to commemorate the trees destroyed in the great storms of 1987 and 1989.

To the west of the wood, Bog Lodge ⓗ is the park's administrative centre, and a base for the Royal Parks Constabulary. Beyond it, the route recrosses Queen's Ride, and the full sweep of this impressive avenue can be appreciated. As you pass Sidmouth Wood, there are spectacular panoramas behind of the City and Docklands.

As you re-enter Pembroke Lodge Gardens, pause to read the rustic

ALL PHOTOS: SUE MORRIS

▲*This view is a reminder that Central London is close, yet still a world away from the magnificent Queen's Ride (below) that sweeps up to White Lodge.*

Deer at Richmond

Richmond Park was first enclosed, as a hunting park, by Charles I, who had a brick wall built around the perimeter in 1637. Traces of medieval fields and drove roads, which survive there to this day, reveal its earlier use for growing crops and as common grazing land.

Oliver Cromwell presented the park to the City of London in 1649, in recognition of the support given him during the Civil War. After the Restoration, however, it was returned to Charles II, who hunted there, as did succeeding monarchs. Deer hunting stopped in the park in Georgian times, yet its character is still very much determined by its resident deer population.

There are two species in the park; about 300 red deer and around 400 fallow deer. They graze the park's grass, and browse the lower branches of the trees, creating the distinctive open landscape and the cropped, flat-bottomed tree shapes.

Supplementary food is provided for them during the winter.

The park is administered today by a superintendent and the Department of National Heritage, but was governed from 1637 to 1910 by a succession of rangers appointed by the reigning monarch.

The most notorious of these rangers was George II's daughter, Princess Amelia, who took up residence at White Lodge in 1751, and set about denying the public access to the park.

This was vigorously contested by the local people, not least the brewer, John Lewis, who became a local hero after several brave legal actions against Amelia eventually re-established the right of free passage in 1758, a right that still enables visitors to enjoy the park today.

Red deer hinds are nervous animals but can be fiercely protective of their young in late spring if you approach them.

memorial to 'James Thomson, poet of nature', and make your way to King Henry VIII's Mound ⓙ. This is probably another prehistoric burial mound; it certainly existed in 1637, when it was known as the King's Standynge. Legend has it that while he was out hunting, Henry VIII stood on the mound to hear a gun fire from the Tower of London to signal the execution of Anne Boleyn.

FAMOUS VIEWPOINT

From the top of the mound, there are spectacular views of south-west London, with glimpses of the River Thames, Ham House and Twickenham Rugby Football Ground. On a clear day, if you turn around and peer towards Sidmouth Wood through the gap in the greenery, you can see St Paul's Cathedral, perfectly framed by the trees, along a protected sight-line.

SILENT POOL

14

SURREY

A downland walk from a tranquil lake to a pretty village

The wooded slopes of the North Downs stretch eastwards from the market town of Farnham to the Channel, terminating as the white cliffs of Dover. These chalk downs are classified as an Area of Outstanding Natural Beauty, and are often regarded as 'London's Countryside'. They are easy to reach from the capital city.

THE HAUNTED POOL

Set in a hollow at the foot of the Downs is Silent Pool **A** where the walk begins. Mystery and legend surround the still, clear waters of Silent Pool. One story tells how one

▲ *The deep, clear waters of Silent Pool are a quiet haven surrounded by trees. (inset) The yellowhammer calls for 'a little bit of bread and cheese'.*

◄ *The picturesque village of Shere is noted for its attractively grouped cottages, some timber-framed.*

FACT FILE

* Silent Pool, near Albury, Surrey. Between Guildford and Dorking on A25

◻= Pathfinder 1226 (TQ 04/14), grid reference TQ 059484

miles 0 1 2 3 4 5 6 7 8 9 10 miles
kms 0 1 2 3 4 5 6 7 8 9 10 11 12 13 14 15 kms

◔ Allow 2½ hours

▭ Easy, with one steep hill climb. Boots recommended for winter and after rain

P Off the A25 at Silent Pool

T British Rail North Downs Line trains stop at Gomshall. From the station, turn right on to the A25 and walk towards Gomshall Mill. Start the walk at Stage 4. Dorking to Guildford buses stop at Silent Pool.

🍺 Pubs and cafés in the villages of Shere and Gomshall

day when out hunting, King John surprised a young girl bathing naked in the pool. She tried to conceal herself by diving deeper and deeper until she drowned. Her brother also drowned attempting to rescue her, and now they are said to haunt the pool by night. In contrast to this sad tale, the poet, Lord Tennyson, regarded Silent Pool as a source of inspiration for his writing.

After leaving the mysterious pool, the route connects with the North Downs Way, a footpath which travels the whole length of the Downs. The walk takes in a short section of this route through woodland before dropping down to Gomshall village, noted for its tannery and Gomshall Mill **B** with its shops, pub and restaurant. The walk returns to Silent Pool via the lovely village of Shere.

BY THE RIVERSIDE

Shere is said to be one of Surrey's prettiest villages. Upper Street and Lower Street are lined by attractive cottages (timber-framed and flint and brick), many of them built during the 17th century. The 12th-century church of St James **C** stands near the village square and fits perfectly into the delightful village scene. Its central tower is topped by a shingled spire. The sparkling waters of Tilling Bourne flow through the centre of the village.

Gomshall is a pretty village on the low, sandy hills south of the Downs.

THE WALK

SILENT POOL – GOMSHALL – SHERE

The walk begins at the car park on the A25 at the entrance for Silent Pool.

▶1 Follow the signposted road for Silent Pool Ⓐ. Go through the gate and take the second right footpath. Silent Pool is the second lake; keep to left-hand side of the pool. At the far end of Silent Pool climb the steps leading upwards. At the top turn left, then right on to the crossing track before field. Follow the track uphill, passing on the right a pillbox (a defensive relic of World War II). As height is gained views open out of Tilling Bourne Valley backed by Winterfold Forest. Storm damage has changed the foreground aspect.

▶2 Near the crest of the Downs the track is crossed by the North Downs Way (at this point a bridleway is marked with the Way's acorn symbol, which will be a useful guide for the next mile). Turn right and follow the North Downs Way for ½ mile (800 metres). A Surrey County Council 'Open Space' sign is soon passed; keep straight on.

▶3 Cross a car park and road, and follow the continuing track which soon reaches a second road. Turn right, then almost immediately left — still on the North Downs Way — taking the broad track for Hollister Farm. Ignore a similar track from the right. Keep straight on. Within ¼ mile (400 metres) there is a junction of several paths adjacent to Hollister Farm. Turn left to pass farm and stables, followed by single bar gate and 'Fire Danger' sign. In ¼ mile (400 metres) the broad track crosses

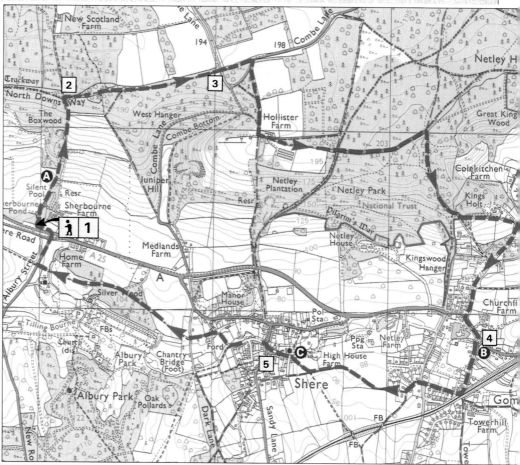

another by a further 'Fire Danger' sign; keep straight on for another ¼ mile (400 metres) until a second crossing track is reached by an acorn sign. Turn right and follow the path which eventually leads down through woodland to a road. Turn right and continue until the road meets the main A25 opposite Gomshall Tanneries. Turn left and soon afterwards turn right into Goose Green (road), by Gomshall Mill Ⓑ. If you are travelling by train to Gomshall station join the walk here at Stage 4.

▶4 Walk along Goose Green (road) through the village. Do not be tempted to pass under railway bridge where road swings right, instead follow to the next junction by Gomshall Lodge. Immediately after the bus stop on the right, keep straight ahead at this

junction to enter Gravelpits Lane. Follow the lane around the left-hand bend and at Gravelpits Farmhouse turn right and follow the enclosed footpath (not the adjacent track leading to gate and field). Soon views open out to the right of the North Downs with Netley House in the distance. Pass through the gate and then in about 300 yards (275 metres) turn right on to a path that passes through a further gate leading to St James' Church in Shere Ⓒ. At the road walk straight ahead to enter the village of Shere.

▶5 Approaching the White Horse public house, cross the road to enter Lower Street beside the Tilling Bourne. Shortly after passing The Prison House on the left (an impressive medieval building of flint and brick with an unusual overhanging

upper storey) Lower Street becomes Rectory Lane and fords the Tilling Bourne. Cross the footbridge over the river. In 200 yards (180 metres) just after 'Ford' sign, fork left on to footpath that starts at The Old Rectory. This narrow path follows alongside a high brick wall to a road. Cross the road and follow the continuing path across a field to a kissing gate. Head for a second kissing gate where path enters woodland. Soon afterwards, a second field is reached by another stile. Cross the field, but bear slightly right, keeping to the right of a flint and brick church (privately owned). Cross a final stile leading to a track that leads to a main road. Turn right and walk to the junction of A25, turn left and carefully cross the busy dual carriageway via the traffic island for car park.

Through woods and fields to the top of a lovely hill

This walk through a relatively untrodden part of Surrey takes you on a gentle climb to Hydon's Ball **A**, a quiet, wooded hilltop with fine views over the surrounding countryside.

The walk starts by St Peter's Church near Hambledon, Surrey. From a sandy undulating bridleway a pleasant view opens out to the left of tree-clad Hydon's Ball, and over your left shoulder is an impressive panorama of rolling fields.

On the right, what appears to be a large and remarkably well-preserved long barrow, or ancient burial mound, is, surprisingly, the bank of the local reservoir.

AT THE SUMMIT

After walking down a leafy, sunken, sandy path and passing a pumping station, the route starts to climb gently through a wood of tall Scots pines, then more steeply to reach the top of Hydon's Ball. At

▲ *Spacious views of the Surrey countryside can be glimpsed through the trees of Hydon's Ball. (inset) The tawny owl is found in woodland areas with scattered mature timber such as farmland and parkland. The bird watches for its prey from a tree perch then swoops silently down to the kill.*
▶ *The disused limekiln near St Peter's Church in Hambledon.*

the summit of Hydon's Ball, a viewpoint on National Trust property, is a large, stone seat commemorating a principal founder of the trust, Octavia Hill, who died in 1912. From here you glimpse through the trees the open countryside beyond.

In summer the tine view from the top is partly obscured by trees on this thickly wooded hill (but there

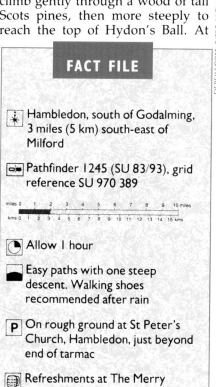

FACT FILE

* Hambledon, south of Godalming, 3 miles (5 km) south-east of Milford

* Pathfinder 1245 (SU 83/93), grid reference SU 970 389

miles 0   1   2   3   4   5   6   7   8   9   10 miles
kms 0 1 2 3 4 5 6 7 8 9 10 11 12 13 14 15 kms

* Allow 1 hour

* Easy paths with one steep descent. Walking shoes recommended after rain

* **P** On rough ground at St Peter's Church, Hambledon, just beyond end of tarmac

* Refreshments at The Merry Harriers (with garden) in Hambledon

THE WALK

HAMBLEDON – HYDON'S BALL

The walk starts by St Peter's Church in Hambledon, Surrey, reached by a very minor road leading out of the village signposted to 'Hambledon Church'.

1 At St Peter's Church there is a signpost to a public footpath and right to a bridleway. Follow the path in the direction of the signposted bridleway. Then, almost immediately, a pleasant view opens up to the left of tree-clad Hydon's Ball **A**. The bridleway is very sandy underfoot.

2 At a T-junction of bridleways, turn left. Almost at once the bridleway bends right, but keep straight ahead and follow the route along a leafy, sunken sandy path.

3 A cross-roads of paths is reached by a small brick structure (a pumping station) on the left. Take the more prominent right-hand path. It soon starts to climb gently, with a wood of tall pines to the right.

4 At a National Trust sign saying 'Hydon's Ball' turn

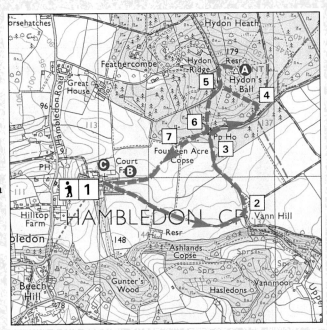

squarely left on to a wide track. Walk along the ascending track through the woods. When the track flattens out ignore a very minor path going right, and when the track forks, take the right fork, which is a much better path. Keep right again for a few steps beyond this point. Then continue the climb to the top of Hydon's Ball. There is a triangulation point here and the large, stone seat commemorating Octavia

Hill. After a rest to admire the view, retrace your steps for about 110 yards (100 metres) on the path on which you came, until you reach a junction of paths, which lies at the bottom of the slope.

5 Ignore the wide path on the left, also the second wide path on the left and the very minor path opposite it on the right. Walk along the tiny path ahead for 12 paces or so until it merges with another path and carry on,

bearing right, gently downhill. The path is fairly narrow and gets progressively steeper. It brings you to the crossroads of paths by the brick pumping station which you passed earlier on the walk.

6 Now turn right through a plantation of sweet chestnut trees on to a path and pass the pumping station to your left. Very soon you will see the churchyard — your final destination — ahead. Bear left on the main path when an indistinct track goes off to the right and pass through a metal kissing gate.

7 Now follow the clear path half-right across the middle of a broad field to another kissing gate. Cross the next field towards the church, just ahead. As you come level with the churchyard, through a wooden gate, notice the ancient limekiln **B** on the left. The church may be locked but make sure you visit the churchyard **C** and look at the remarkable old yews. It is said that the yews here may have been growing in the churchyard when the Magna Carta was signed by King John in 1215.

are fairly good views even then). It is a walk that is especially suitable early in the year when the trees are bare, and in frosty weather the mainly sandy paths and bridleways are less likely to be muddy.

THE HAMBLEDON KILN

Near the end of the walk, almost level with St Peter's churchyard, there is an ancient limekiln **B**. Until fairly recent times, lime — produced from chalk — was the universal agricultural fertiliser. The well-preserved Hambledon Kiln, resembling a small tunnel in a brick wall, was in use until the last century. When in use the fire would have burned about 5 feet (1.5 metres) within the tunnel.

ANCIENT YEWS

The small, hillside church of St Peter was rebuilt in 1840 and inside little remains of the earlier church. To look around the church you may need to ask for a key, but the churchyard must not be missed. Here there are two tremendous yew trees **C**. One is a fine straight tree of 18 feet (5.4 metres) round, the other is a mighty 30 feet (9 metres) in circumference. Its eerie hollow could hold as many as 12 people, and children simply love to stand inside. A local legend says that if you walk around the inside of this tree 13 times widdershins (anti-clockwise), a witch will appear. It certainly feels possible!

The great yews in St Peter's churchyard may date back to the 13th century.

A walk in gentle countryside threaded by streams

Punctuated by many points of historic interest, this walk is never far from attractive waterside scenery. It takes you through pleasant countryside across the waterways of the River Wey. You visit Wisley and its famous Royal Horticultural Society Gardens and appealing Norman church, and cross a newly constructed golf course. There is also an opportunity to relax at a canal-side pub before making your way to the roaring water at Walsham Flood Gates.

Ripley **A**, an old coaching village, has been a popular venue for cricketers and cyclists since the last century. And the green here is reputed to be the largest village green in the country. The old way from the village to Ockham Mill (Holly Bush Lane) is marked on a map dated 1769. Ockham Mill **B** was built in 1862 by the Earl of Lovelace and remains essentially unchanged. There has been a mill on this site since 1297.

FAMOUS GARDENS

The Royal Horticultural Society Gardens **C** at Wisley attract thousands of visitors each year. But millions more people are familiar with the grounds through gardening programmes on television.

Wisley Church **D** is an unspoilt example of Norman architecture, with a Norman chancel arch and chancel windows. Opposite the church, the fields are the site of a neolithic settlement where flints and pottery have been found.

The canal-side Anchor Inn may look familiar. It was frequently shown during the *Adrian Mole* series on television. Nearby Pyrford Lock **E**, with its marina, is a popular spot

Seven Acres lake is set in the beautiful gardens at Wisley. The variety of the many different and colourful species of plant life grown here is a delight to all.

▲ *The peaceful waters of the River Wey reflect the lush trees lining the banks. The river goes on to join the Thames at Weybridge. (inset) A male blackbird, recognisable by his striking yellow beak, guards his territory.*

with anglers and river people. In 1651 the Wey Navigation was built to link Guildford with the Thames and London. Further along the route, Pyrford Place **F** has an imposing building on the bank with a domed roof — a 17th-century summer house in an attractive setting.

At Walsham Flood Gates **G** the Wey Navigation and the River Wey separate, rejoining close to the river's mouth at Weybridge. Walsham Lock is some 12–15 (4–5 metres) above the river. Further on, Dunsborough Park **H** has gardens that are sometimes open to the public and the mansion is home to former actress, Florence Desmond.

FACT FILE

☀ Ripley, near Woking, Surrey

▭ Pathfinder 1206 (TQ 05/15), grid reference TQ 054569

miles 0 1 2 3 4 5 6 7 8 9 10 miles
kms 0 1 2 3 4 5 6 7 8 9 10 11 12 13 14 15 kms

◑ Allow 2 hours

▬ Easy, flat terrain. Likely to be muddy in winter

T The 715 Green Line Bus or train to Guildford station where there is a regular bus service

P Car park on Ripley Green off the B2215

🍴 Refreshments in the High Street and by canal at The Anchor Inn

WC By car park

THE WALK

RIPLEY – WISLEY GARDENS – WALSHAM LOCK

The walk begins from the car park in the village of Ripley, just off the A3 about 4½ miles from Woking.

➡ From the car park at Ripley **A**, continue along a gravel path with cottages on your right. Bear left past another small car park and pass between a cricket ground and pavilion. On reaching practice nets, bear left towards a gap in the trees ahead and continue on a narrow path. Maintain this direction by going over several crossing paths. Other paths come in from both left and right. Always keeping the large Ripley Green on your left and the densest area of trees to your right, pass two seats on your right and head for a waymarked post leading you into woods. Soon you go over a footbridge and join what was once a byway: Holly Bush Lane. Continue over another bridge to emerge on a tarmac lane.

➡ **2** Turn left for about 100 yards (90 metres) to see Ockham Mill **B**, watching out for a footpath sign on the right to which you should return. Follow the path past bungalows, over a stile and along an enclosed stretch between fields. Go over a roadway and a stile, making for another stile (collapsed) into the woods ahead. Shortly you will reach Wisley Royal Horticultural Society Gardens **C**. Return to continue the walk, following a fenced path with the River Wey on your left. A stile leads out to Wren Cottage. Turn right here to reach the entrance to Wisley Gardens.

➡ **3** Turn left along the footway, following the lane for 100 yards (90 metres) or so and, where it bears left, cross the road to maintain direction for about ⅓ mile (600 metres) on a well-defined, bracken-lined, public footpath on Wisley Common. Later you will see a field on your left. At a fork by a signpost keep left and left again at the next one. As the roar of the M25 traffic becomes more apparent you will reach a main crossing track where you turn left. Go over a stile, ignore the farm track and maintain direction over farmland, soon passing a row of trees. You come to a concreted driveway on which you turn left to reach the lane that you left earlier. (This has no pavement so take care.)

➡ **4** Turn right and continue along the lane, crossing the River Wey by the Wisley Bridge, for about another ⅓ mile (600 metres). Follow the lane as it curves around farm buildings and then turn into Wisley Churchyard **D**.

➡ **5** Immediately after passing the church turn left towards an old barn alongside which is a path leading over a stile and into a field. Bear left towards an earth bridge and a wooden footbridge over ditches, then continue ahead on a right of way across the golf course. Turn right and continue carefully to cross the golf course. Your path brings you out opposite the Anchor Inn and Pyrford Lock **E**.

➡ **6** Remaining on the same bank, go past the bridge over the Wey Navigation to join the towpath. Continue along this for ½ mile (800 metres). To your right you will see Pyrford Place Farm and Pyrford Green. Eventually, on the opposite bank, you will see the grounds of Pyrford Place **F**. In another ½ mile (800 metres) you will hear the roar of water as it passes through Walsham Flood Gates **G**.

➡ **7** Cross over the bridge by the weir and leave the canal, continuing on an enclosed path which leads you back to the large field by Ripley Green. Turn right on to a gravel road with houses on your right and when this bears left, continue ahead on a small path past a magnificent mansion with a topiary garden: Dunsborough Park **H**. After passing a children's play area, turn left and continue back to the car park where the walk ends.

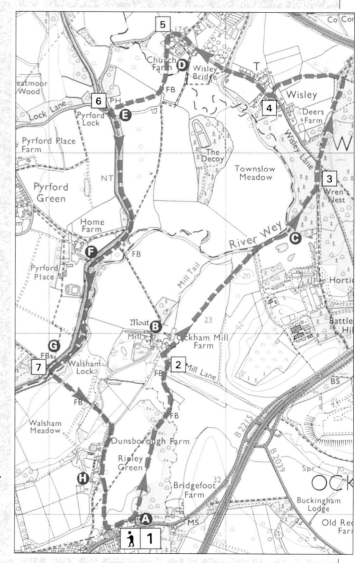

A mini-waterfall in the heart of Surrey. The torrents of water rushing through Walsham Flood Gates can be heard long before walkers reach the weir.

S & O MATHEWS

LITTLE SWITZERLAND

AA PICTURE LIBRARY INSET: ALAN STEWART

From a tranquil lake to the highest point in south-east England

This woodland walk in a secluded part of Surrey known as Little Switzerland combines a wealth of history with some of the finest scenery in the south of England. The walk also takes in Leith Hill, the highest point in south-east England, offering fine views across the Weald.

A QUIET VALLEY

Only a few minutes from the car-park at the start of the walk is Friday Street lake **A**, nestling in a circle of tree-clad hills. Until late Tudor times this now peaceful valley resounded with the clamour of an iron foundry, its hammers powered by water from the lake and its furnaces fed by charcoal from the surrounding forest. By the 17th century it had acquired its present tranquil aspect and the diarist John Evelyn, whose family owned near-by Wotton Manor, fished in its clear depths. A passionate lover of trees, he wrote *Sylva*, the influential book on arboriculture, in 1664. Evelyn

commenced the planting of many unusual species in the woods near to his family home.

Along the lane past the lake is the Stephan Langton **B**, an inviting pub set among a handful of cottages. The name and portrait of this cleric on the inn-sign recall the local tradition that the great archbishop was born in this tiny village. A copy of the 13th-century Magna Carta

FACT FILE

- Friday Street, 3 miles (4.8 km) south-west of Dorking on A25

- Pathfinder 1226 (TQ 04/14), grid reference TQ 126457

  miles 0 1 2 3 4 5 6 7 8 9 10 miles
  kms 0 1 2 3 4 5 6 7 8 9 10 11 12 13 14 15 kms

- Allow 2½ hours

- Easy with one steep hill

- **P** Car park 150 yards (140 metres) west of Friday Street

- Stephan Langton pub at Friday Street. Leith Hill Tower is open for refreshments only at weekends in winter from 9.00 am to 4.00 pm and later in the summer months

▲ *The diarist John Evelyn claimed that it was possible to see 12 or 13 counties from the top of Leith Hill. (inset) The colourful but poisonous fly agaric fungi are found in birch woodlands.*

▼ *The big pond at Friday Street*

ALAN STEWART

that he witnessed hangs in the bar.

Entering the woodland, the path runs beside the little stream that feeds the lake. The woods are a mixture of beech and pine, with some oaks and mountain ash. Height is gradually gained and, emerging at the top of Leith Hill, the panorama of the Weald opens out below. At a height of 967 feet (290 metres), this is the highest point in south-east England, affording a view of the sea through the

THE WALK

FRIDAY STREET-LEITH HILL

The walk starts at Friday Street car park.

1 Turn right on the road outside car park and at the lake **A**, turn right with the lake now on your left, past the Stephan Langton pub **B**. Continue ahead along a track through woods with a small stream on your left. Ignore all paths to left and right and when this track reaches a road, turn left along the road for 75 yards (70 metres) to a cottage. This is Abinger Bottom **C**.

2 When the road bears left, go straight ahead along a bridleway between two cottages. Follow this track, which continues gently uphill, for 1/2 mile (800 metres) to a fork with a signpost; fork right here and, crossing a drive, continue on the path opposite to a road. Turn left on to the road and after 60 yards (55 metres) when a road enters from the left, take the bridleway on the left beside the fire hazard warning.

The bridleway rises gently through bracken, pines and heather and in a little over 1/4 mile (400 metres) when the bridleway swings sharply left, continue straight ahead along a narrower path. Ignoring all paths to left and right, continue for a further 1/4 mile (400 metres) until the path broadens and forks. Take the right fork and in 100 yards (90 metres) on joining a wide crossing track, turn left. Leith Hill Tower is now visible ahead **D**.

3 Leave the tower by the north-west fenced path which runs slightly uphill and when this forks after 100 yards (90 metres), keep right. Ignore crosspaths immediately after the right fork, The path soon forks again and here bear left.

After about 1/4 mile (400 metres), a wide crossing track is joined in a clearing in the bracken; turn right along this track and continue gently downhill, ignoring turnings to the right. When the track divides, keep right along the lower path. When this meets a gravel drive, turn right and in 100 yards (90 metres), take a path on the left which leads downhill among trees, in a gradually widening valley, to the hamlet of Broadmoor **E**.

4 About 50 yards (45 metres) past the telephone box, turn left on a path running uphill, next to the parish notice board. Bear right when the path forks. The path forks again within 200 yards (180 metres) ; keep left and continue uphill to a slightly wider track, continuing uphill to a road. Cross the road and in 75 yards (70 metres), cross a second road to a path opposite. Follow this steep path downhill to Friday Street lake. Turn left on meeting the road to reach the car park at end of walk.

Shoreham gap to the south, and of St Paul's Cathedral through the Mole valley gap to the north.

The 65 foot (20 metre) tower **D**, originally named Prospect Place, was built by Richard Hull of Leith Hill Place in 1766. Friends were entertained in the upper room where telescopes were provided to enjoy views over the beautiful countryside of Surrey.

TOWER ON THE HILL

When the tower is open, the energetic can climb to the top, which brings you above 1,000 feet (300 metres), the minimum height at which a mere hill becomes a real mountain. On the top of the tower are indicators of distant viewpoints, presented in memory of the famous rambler, 'Walker Miles', a founder of rambling clubs with the reputation of being a great countryman.

Leaving the tower, the walk crosses some of the heathland on top of Leith Hill and then follows a lovely woodland track leading gently downhill to the pretty hamlet of Broadmoor **E**. A short, but exhilarating uphill climb then follows before the final descent through Severells Copse to the lake and car park at Friday Street.

◀ *The tower on Leith Hill offers magnificent views of fine walking country. (above) This includes paths through beautiful, secluded woodland.*

SURREY

Step back in time on a scenic route once used by medieval pilgrims

Good views, delightful scenery and interesting sights will be your reward on this walk through the gentle Surrey countryside. The area offers the outstanding natural beauty of the North Downs and there are many historical and architectural attractions along the route.

Starting from the church noticeboard atop St Martha's Hill, the walk takes you through Chantry Woods **A**, eventually leading down to Chantry Cottage **B**. The corpses of plague victims are reputed to have been kept here in the 17th century.

An extension on the south-western corner of the route takes you to Shalford Mill **C**, which dates from the 18th century and is now in the care of the National Trust. The mill operated until 1914 and most of the machinery remains intact, so it is well worth a visit.

Looking back from this point, you can see the copper spire of Shalford Church, a Victorian building on the

FACT FILE

- St Martha's, near Chilworth, 2 miles (3.2 km) south-east of Guildford on A248
- Pathfinder 1226 (TQ 04/14), grid reference TQ 022484

miles 0 1 2 3 4 5 6 7 8 9 10 miles
kms 0 1 2 3 4 5 6 7 8 9 10 11 12 13 14 15 kms

- Allow 4, 2¾ or 2 hours, depending on walk chosen
- Moderately energetic, with a steep climb up St Martha's Hill. Relatively few stiles
- **P** Car park off Halfpenny Lane
- **T** Good public transport from Guildford to Stage 2 of walk, or to Chilworth for Stage 4.
- Village shop and Drummond Arms in Albury, Sea Horse pub in Shalford and Percy Arms in Chilworth
- **WC** By Youth Camp (longest and shortest walks only)

There were three watermills in Shalford in the 11th century. Today there is only one — the 18th-century Shalford Mill.

▲ *A view of St Martha's Hill from the village of Chilworth. The water-loving Orange balsam (inset) was introduced from North America and cultivated in greenhouses before escaping to the wild.*

THE WALK

ST MARTHA'S – SHALFORD – ALBURY

The walk starts by the church noticeboard in the car park on St Martha's Hill.

■➤ Facing church noticeboard, take a path on the left and go forward to a wide track; turn right; follow a sandy gully out to Halfpenny Lane and turn left. If taking the 5½ mile (8.8 km) walk, go down the lane for almost ½ mile (800 metres) and, just after a farm gate, look for a footpath sign on the right. You rejoin the walk at Stage 3.

Continue downhill for some 50 yards (45 metres), then turn right at a sign to the North Downs Way into Chantry Woods Ⓐ. Immediately bear left at a fork on to a wide track through the woods and continue straight ahead to the wooden buildings of a Youth Camp site. Bear left, then right, following the path along the top of the hillside and keeping woods to the right.

Around ½ mile (800 metres) past the camp site, just before the path dips, turn right by a red-painted nature trail post. Ignore the immediate left turn but soon bear left on a wide footpath into the woods. At a T-junction turn left, soon passing an open area on the right. At a fork bear right to maintain a westerly direction. Wind downhill to the next fork and continue straight ahead, later veering left down to the valley bottom and to the white Chantry Cottage Ⓑ, where you come out through a gate.

■2 Turn left along the permissive bridleway, follow it to a road, turn left and continue for a few yards to

a stile on the left. If you wish to visit Shalford Mill Ⓒ do not go over the stile but continue ahead. Cross a lane to a stile and follow a field edge to the mill. (The Seahorse pub is nearby on the main road.) After visiting the mill, retrace your steps to the point where you left the main route. Cross the stile and continue straight ahead on a path between fields. When you reach a stile on the right, look back to enjoy the view, noting the spire of Shalford Church on the left and Guildford Cathedral on the right.

Continue along the field, keeping the hedgerow to the right, and pass Manor Farmhouse. Turn right over a stile, then go left to continue in your previous direction. Pass the barns of Little Halfpenny Farm and eventually go through a gate leading back to Halfpenny Lane Ⓓ. Turn right to find a footpath sign.

■3 Turn right downhill on an enclosed path until you see a pill box Ⓔ on the far side of a field on the left. At the bottom you meet Halfpenny Lane once again and turn left along it. When the lane turns sharply left, go straight ahead on a tarmac bridleway to

Chilworth Manor Ⓕ. From the gateway, bear right on a track in a field on the right to soon find a path leading uphill on the left.

■4 Those taking the 4 mile (6.4 km) walk should turn left along the path and continue between young trees, soon climbing steeply up St Martha's Hill to the church. Continue the walk from Stage 10.

To continue the full walk carry on along the track, which later becomes the Downs Link Path Ⓖ. Passing another pill box on the left, continue to Long Furrow Farm entrance on the left and make your first crossing over the River Tillingbourne Ⓗ. Very shortly turn right through a wicket gate, bearing left into woods and soon turn left by a high bank of earth. Keep on this path, with the canal on your right; to the left are the ruins of the gunpowder works Ⓙ.

Turn right over a bridge on to a tarmacked bridleway and you will come to the main road at Chilworth. Those arriving by train at Chilworth may start the walk here. (The Percy Arms is just ¼ mile (400 metres) down the road on the right.) Cross

the road and go over a railway bridge.

■5 Fork left on a public footpath into a field, heading for a solitary oak tree. Go up an embankment and maintain direction across another field. There is a good view of Albury Church Ⓚ on the left. Go over a stile into a field, turn right and head for a row of trees. Continue towards a house in the distance. Go over a stile and soon bear left, passing between farm buildings, then cross a tributary of the Tillingbourne and eventually emerge on Blackheath Lane.

■6 Turn left uphill, shortly going under a railway bridge, and continue along the lane for about ½ mile (800 metres) until it joins a road. Turn right here and walk on for 100 yards (90 metres) or so if you want to visit Albury church Ⓚ.

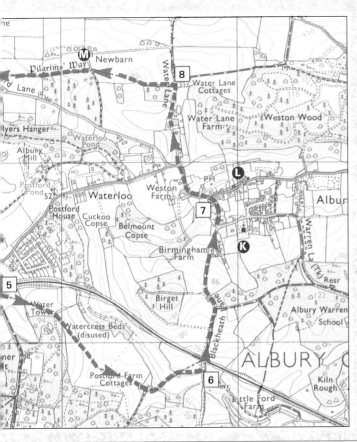

Continue ahead along the pavement to reach the main street in Albury **L**. (The village store is in front of you and the Drummond Arms a few yards down to the right.)

7 Turn left along the busy road, taking care if you have children with you. Cross the river again and, where the road turns sharply left, cross over to Water Lane. Keep on this for about 500 yards (450 metres) until you reach a bridleway sign on the left.

8 Turn sharply left up a slope on to the Pilgrims' Way **M** with good views on the right up to Newlands Corner on Albury Downs. Go along the left side of a field, keeping the distant Newbarn Farm slightly to the right. Turn right at a T-junction, heading towards farm buildings, but long

before you reach them follow the sandy path with woods on the left around to the left. Later, pass between fences and come out to a lane where you turn right for 100 yards (90 metres) or so.

9 Turn left through a small parking area and continue straight ahead on another very sandy track which winds its way gradually uphill. Passing close by a pill box, you reach the North Downs Way. This soon forks left, but continue ahead uphill, ignoring all other turnings, to reach St Martha's Church **N**.

10 From the church proceed in your previous, westerly direction, soon rejoining the North Downs Way coming in from the left. Descend this pine-clad slope passing an open area on the right, to return to car park.

site of a Domesday church, and the imposing outline of Guildford Cathedral. The village of Shalford itself is reputed to be the model for Vanity Fair in *The Pilgrim's Progress*.

Returning to the main route, the walk continues through undulating countryside to Halfpenny Lane **D**. This derives its name from the time when tolls were levied on cattle drovers using it as a short cut over the hill to Guildford market.

◀ *The beginning point of the Downs Way link footpaths on St Martha's Hill, It joins the North Downs and South Downs Ways.*
▼ *Many of the old buildings in Albury village were designed by the Gothic-Revival architect, Pugin.*

A short way further on is a pill box **E** — one of the World War II fortifications erected in anticipation of a German invasion. There are plans to turn them into roosts and hibernation sites for bats.

ST MARTHA'S HILL

Chilworth Manor **F** was a monastery in the 11th century, listed in the Domesday Book. Destroyed in the reign of Henry VIII, the building passed to the Duchess of Marlborough in 1725. Now privately owned, the house and grounds are opened to the public on several days each year.

Stately Chilworth Manor stands on the site of a monastery. It was destroyed in the 16th century when Henry VIII became head of the Church of England.

Guildford Cathedral

of spaciousness and light.

Yet another personal contribution, and an important feature of the cathedral, are the hundreds of kneeling mats, nearly all different and worked by some 800 or more men, women and children. Blue, being Guildford's colour, predominates. To provide a unifying link, all the kneelers except those in the Lady Chapel, are divided diagonally; the lower half suggests Stag Hill and the upper half the blue sky.

The golden angel glistens above the tower of Guildford Cathedral on Stag Hill. The cathedral's simplified Gothic interior (below) is light and spacious.

In a perfect location, high above the town on Stag Hill, stands Guildford's Cathedral of the Holy Spirit, its shining Golden Angel rising above the tower and catching the sunlight.

An open competition for the design of the cathedral in 1932 was won by Sir Edward Maufe. The foundation stone was laid in 1936; but war interrupted the work and it was not resumed until 1952. The cathedral was eventually consecrated on 17th May 1961.

The unpretentious exterior is of red brick, using local clay from Stag Hill. Many people 'bought' these bricks, thus making a modest but very personal contribution to the building. The clean lines of the interior are enhanced by cream Doulting limestone and fine Purbeck paving stones, which create a feeling

Just beyond the manor on St Martha's Hill, Downs Link **G** joins the North Downs Way with the South Downs Way. It runs for 30 miles (48 km) to Steyning.

Passing the River Tillingbourne **H**, a network of streams where a pretty plant, orange balsam, grows, you come to Chilworth Gunpowder Works **J**. Dating back to 1580, the works flourished until a serious explosion in 1901. Thereafter they declined and even the munition demands of World War I could not save them.

THE MEDIEVAL PILGRIMS

Winding south-eastwards, the route turns north up Blackheath Lane to Albury Church **K**. Built in the 19th century by a local landowner, it was intended to be a copy of a church in Thaon, Normandy; however, it was mistakenly built of red brick instead of stone.

The village of Albury **L** is noted for its extravagant, Tudor-style chimneys designed by Pugin in the early-19th century.

Heading northwards, the walk joins the Pilgrims' Way **M**, a route followed by medieval pilgrims travelling to the shrine of St Thomas à Becket in Canterbury. This ancient route intersects with the more recently created North Downs Way, a 150-mile (240-km) footpath from Farnham to Dover. It was opened in 1978 by Dr Donald Coggan, then Archbishop of Canterbury.

The final stretch of the walk passes the 11th-century St Martha's Church **N**. The original chapel was damaged by a gunpowder explosion in 1763 and not rebuilt until 1850. There is a traditionally held belief that early Christians were martyred here around 600 AD by pagan

The walled churchyard and 11th-century church of St Martha's were built on a site where Christians were martyred.

Saxons, so the name 'Martha' may be a corruption of 'martyr'. In the churchyard is the grave of the French-born actress Yvonne Arnaud who gave her name to Guildford's theatre, opened in 1965.

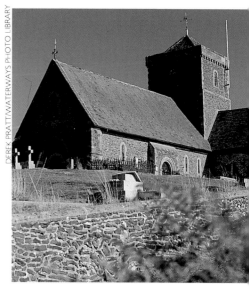

SURREY

◀ Until the 1930s, most of Headley Heath was open heathland. The siskin (inset) winters in birch and alder trees.

ALAN STEWART. INSET: SWIFT PICTURE LIBRARY

house, a path through a pastoral landscape leads to a tiny wood, at the end of which is the Heath. A moderately steep and stony path gives way to a surfaced drive, followed before long by a grassy path, a sandy track and a narrow, stony path. These changes of surface underfoot continue for the rest of the walk. The scenery differs even more as the route goes through a great variety of vegetation.

THE FOREST

After a climb to an open, grassy space, a steep descent follows down a path of wooden steps. On the way, a breathtaking view **B** of a deeply wooded valley opens up on the left.

From the foot of the hill another climb — but a gentle one — begins, and another valley view appears to the right **C**. Behind are delightful views towards Box Hill.

Headley, as it appears today, owes much to the effects of World War II, when intensive tank training disturbed the soil and encouraged the growth of birch. Birch growth is only a transitional stage in the development of forest and, over the years, longer-lived hardwoods such as oak and beech will take over.

FACT FILE

✱ Headley, 3 miles (4 km) east of Leatherhead

▱ Pathfinder 1206 (TQ 05/15) and 1207 (25/35), grid reference TQ 205539

miles 0 1 2 3 4 5 6 7 8 9 10 miles
kms 0 1 2 3 4 5 6 7 8 9 10 11 12 13 14 15 kms

◔ Allow 2¹/₂ hours

▬ A fairly strenuous walk with numerous changes of level. Paths and tracks are sometimes stony. Muddy in parts after rain. Strong footwear recommended. Not suitable for young children

P In the National Trust car park on the B2033. Small parking fee charged (no change given in meter)

▦ The Cock pub in Headley. Refreshment kiosk in car park

T An approximately hourly bus service from Leatherhead on weekdays only. (Join at Station Road, if travelling by train). Alight at The Cock in Headley and start (and finish) at Stage 3 in the instructions on page 2, overleaf

A walk along pleasant field paths and beautiful heathland with fine views

This walk on wild and lovely heathland is preceded by a stroll on field paths to Headley Church **A**. Headley Heath, near Box Hill, covers 530 acres (141 hectares). The land was originally grazed by sheep. Today, under the management of the National Trust, the heath's various habitats are maintained for the benefit of a wide variety of flora and fauna.

Headley Heath is rich in wildlife and attractive plants. There is a variety of interesting birds to look out for — woodpeckers, linnets, pipits, goldfinches and siskins. Heathers and ling are widespread and there are even orchids and rock roses.

The walk starts from the Trust's car park. A short walk across a bracken-covered corner of the Heath leads to the late-Victorian church of St Mary the Virgin.

Opposite the nearby Cock public

▶ *The church in Headley features panelling from Newgate Prison.*

ALAN STEWART

THE WALK

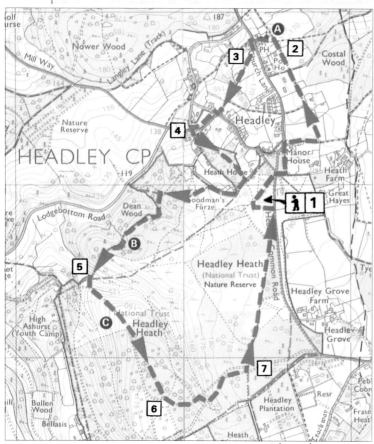

HEADLEY HEATH

The walk begins from the National Trust car park opposite the cricket ground on the B2033.

1 Walk away from the refreshment kiosk to the inner car park. Pass through a gap in the wall and turn immediately sharp right on to a clear path, which bends left, then right. When it soon divides take the right fork and, when it divides again, turn to the road. Cross the road half-left and turn right into the left-hand of two private roads. Turn immediately left on to a path through the trees, parallel with the road. When the path (sometimes muddy) almost converges with a road, walk along a driveway, signposted 'Webb Cottage and Webbs Farm', bear with it as it curves right and go towards a house. Before reaching it, turn left along a waymarked footpath. (Be careful of nettles that restrict the path in summer and autumn). Cross a stile and turn left along a grassy path which continues over numerous stiles and eventually leads to Headley Church **A**.

2 Walk just beyond the north-east entrance/exit to the churchyard to view the grandstand of Epsom Racecourse. Enter the churchyard and make your way (respecting the graves) to the main exit and come to the road by the Cock public house.

3 Cross the road diagonally leftwards from the pub, and enter a track by the bus stop. Walk along for about 1/4 mile (400 metres). On reaching a road, turn right and almost immediately turn right again on to a rough driveway. After a short distance, turn left and take the right-hand of two paths opposite a large house. Soon the path drops down to another minor road. Turn left for a few paces to the road and cross to a National Trust 'Headley Heath' sign.

4 Here, take the minor path to the left of the sign. The path gradually climbs. Ignore a path to the right and continue uphill until the route is crossed by an asphalt drive. Then turn right on to the drive. Continue on this drive as it bends right, ignoring a path to the left and, when it comes to Heath House, bear left across a sandy track and take the grassy path that faces the house. Bear right on to a wider grassy track. Pass over a sandy track, then turn left on to the next sandy track and drop downhill. Ignore a path on the right that drops towards a ditch. Pass over a crosstrack. The path soon narrows and, in a dip, meets another path curving in from the left and curving away to the right. Take the right-hand direction uphill. The path rises, then later drops into a deep dip and up the other side. At the top on a fairly open, grassy patch, ignore the wide track to the left which seems to start from here. Now be careful! Turn half-right and make your way over the grass until you come to a path curving leftwards on the right-hand side of a large clump of trees and bushes. Go down some wooden steps. A remarkable view of a glorious wooded valley **B** opens up to the left as you descend the steep hillside. At the bottom of the hill you reach a wide, stony track. Turn right on it and continue for a very short distance before going left through an iron barrier.

5 As the grassy way gradually rises, views open up on either side across thickly wooded valleys **C** Near the top of the hill a wide space spreads out, first to the left and then to the right. Soon, a grassy track curves to the right and then bends left, but ignore this and carry on, keeping the clump of trees to your right.

6 When the trees begin to close in a little you come to a small, open space from which six paths radiate. Take the second path to the left, clearly the major one. Not long after this the path starts to drop into a dip and there is a crosstrack before the bottom. Turn right here on to a very muddy bridleway. At a T-junction turn left, then bear right at the next T-junction (with a junction of several paths to be seen on the left).

7 When you come to a wide crosstrack, turn left. On reaching a small pond on the left, surrounded by a wire fence, pass to the left of the pond and walk round it. Take the path ahead, through a silver birch wood. At a T-junction, turn right and after just a few paces, continue on the path ahead, ignoring a path to the left and the track to the right. Continue to walk ahead, ignoring minor paths left and right. When you come to a junction of paths walk on, bear slightly to the left and return to the car park.

A riverside walk through hamlets and past an historic school

Godalming, the town in which this walk commences, has plenty to attract the visitor. On the walk you will come across many points of interest with histories going back several hundred years. These include ancient bridges, built by monks to stand the test of time, and an estate village which creates a picture of life as it would have been 200 years ago.

The original St Peter and St Paul Church **Ⓐ** was recorded in 1086 as part of the estate of Rannulf Flambard who came from Normandy to join the court of

FACT FILE

- ✴ Town centre, Godalming, Surrey

- ⌦ Pathfinder 1225 (SU 84/94), grid reference SU970440

  miles 0 1 2 3 4 5 6 7 8 9 10 miles
  kms 0 1 2 3 4 5 6 7 8 9 10 11 12 13 14 15 kms

- ◔ 2 hours for the short walk; 3½ hours for the long walk

- ▭ Easy walking with one steady climb and a steep descent, few stiles and very little mud even after rain. There is no footbridge across the A3, so the longer walk will not be suitable for young children or anyone who cannot manage a short, quick sprint

- Ⓟ Crown Court public car park behind Waitrose store in High Street

- Ⓣ Godalming station is close to the beginning of walk. Frequent service on Waterloo-Portsmouth line. Buses from Guildford and surrounding villages

- 🍴 The Stag public house and the Cyder House Inn

▲ *The River Wey meanders through peaceful Surrey meadows. The small tortoiseshell butterfly (right) produces two broods each year, one in June and another later in August and September.*

William the Conqueror. The present church was built on the same site as the original in the 1860s. During excavations the foundations of a chancel and nave revealed a total of 11 skeletons buried within the walls.

Westbrook Place **Ⓑ** was the home of Sir Theophilus Oglethorpe in the 17th century. His son, General James Oglethorpe, was the founder of the State of Georgia in the USA.

THE OLD SCHOOL

Charterhouse School **Ⓒ**, founded in London in 1611, moved to Godalming in 1872. The impressive buildings greatly enhanced the town and caused it gradually to expand to accommodate the new residents that were attracted here.

The hamlet of Upper Eashing **Ⓓ**

consists of farmhouses that have now become desirable modern residences. The road through the hamlet leads down to the famous double Eashing Bridges **Ⓕ**.

There are several of these bridges over the Wey between Guildford and Farnham, built as a series by the monks of Waverley Abbey in the 13th century. They are now in the care of the National Trust and long may they remain as a reminder of how well our ancestors built, with none of the technological advan-

DEREK FORSS

A. J. ROBERTS/FRANK LANE PICTURE AGENCY

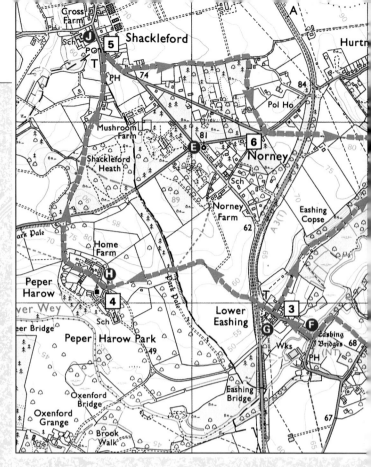

THE WALK

GODALMING – PEPER HAROW – SHACKLEFORD

The walk begins at the Crown Court public car park behind the Waitrose store in Godalming High Street. If you are entering the town via the Town Bridge, follow the signs for Crown Court.

1 Facing away from the High Street, leave the car park through the opening in the wall at the top left-hand corner. Cross the road and continue past a children's recreation area. At a crossing path, turn left and, keeping the church **A** on your right, come out to a road. Cross over to Station Approach opposite and soon bear right into Westbrook Road. Go under the railway, continue ahead and soon pass Westbrook Place **B** on your left. Continue steadily uphill on this surfaced bridleway and over to your right you should be able to see the spire of Charterhouse School **C** on the skyline. When the surfaced track turns sharply left, you continue ahead through a wooden gate, past a house on your right, and reach another gate. Bearing slightly right,

maintain direction for another ½ mile (800 metres) during which you will pass some farm buildings on your way to reach a road.

2 Turn right along the road, again noticing the Charterhouse spire on the skyline to the right. Stay on the road as it turns left through Upper Eashing **D** and just before you reach a white house on the right (Dean Cottage), turn right over a stile by a public footpath sign. Continue straight across a field, close to the edge of a steep slope, and you will see the spire of Shackleford Church **E** on the horizon ahead. A stile leads you down some steps through woods (take care as there are nettles here), with the River Wey down on your right. The Eashing Bridges **F** soon come into view as you reach a road. (For refreshments continue ahead on the road to The Stag public house by the mill building.) To continue the walk turn right over the bridges and through Lower Eashing **G** to a bridleway sign on your right.

3 If you wish to take a shorter walk, turn right on to a made-up bridleway, passing stables, and going over an open area at first. As the road bears left, go straight ahead, through a gate, and take the sandy path that leads through the woods. Maintain direction on this path for a little over 1 mile (1.6 km) to reach Stage 7.

If you wish to complete the full walk, continue ahead and, just before you reach

the edge of the busy A3 London-Portsmouth trunk road, turn right on a track leading across a footbridge. On the other side go through a metal gate and turn right along a sandy bridleway. At the top of a field turn left towards a row of conifers. Turn right through a gate and, almost immediately, left through a strip of woods to a stile. Continue straight across a field, keeping to the left of three cedar trees, and pass a large barn on your right.

◄*Between Westbrook Place and Charterhouse, the walk passes through idyllic pastoral scenery.*

ALAN STEWART

tages that we take for granted today. Notice the well-shaped cutwaters taking the flow of the tide; they are rounded on the downstream side to prevent eddying and eventual wearing down of the piers.

A resident of Lower Eashing **G** from a century or two past would probably find that it looks similar now to the way it did 200 years ago. There has been a mill here since Domesday and, if you look carefully as you walk through, you will find evidence of the site of the former

smithy's forge. A modern bridge carries the A3 over the river a ¼ mile (400 metres) below Eashing. During its building, skeletons were found with a Roman hairpin lying near the head of one of them.

STATELY SPIRE

Located a little way from the village itself is Shackleford Church **E**. Its magnificent spire was built in 1865 by Sir George Gilbert Scott.

Just before arriving at Peper Harow **H**, you pass a group of cedars of Lebanon which were planted as seedlings in 1735, when the estate village as you see it today was formed. The present mansion,

Keeping this field to your left, continue for ⅓ mile (530 metres) and, at a footpath/bridleway signpost, turn right into woods and reach a road by a junction.

▶ Cross the road and bear left onto a public footpath leading along the left-hand edge of a recreation field. A metal kissing gate takes you out to the busy A3 again which you cross (with great care). Another kissing gate leads you into a field which you cross, heading for the third pylon from the left and a stile. Maintain your easterly direction, going diagonally left across the field to another stile in the trees. (If this field is in crop you may prefer to turn left to the field corner and then go right along the fence to the stile on your left.) Bear left and then right downhill on a stepped path **K**. At the bottom of the path, turn left and continue for a short distance until you reach a crossing track.

▶ Turn right and soon go through the left of two gates, passing a house on your right. This enclosed

path takes you through a metal barrier and the River Wey **L** comes into view again on your right. Continue on this narrow path for about another ⅓ mile (530 metres), through another barrier and onto a residential road on which you continue for a little over 300 yards (270 metres).

▶ Turn right onto a hedged public footpath signposted to Godalming. After going over a footbridge, the tarred path bears left alongside the river again. The path leads across the entrance to a business headquarters, and out to a road where you turn right to go under the railway. Almost immediately, at a footpath sign, bear right across a car park and onto a wooden footbridge, with Boarden Bridge **M** on your left, and return to the road. Turn left over the road to pass the cloister **N** on your left and the church on your right. At a T-junction in the path, turn right and soon left and right again back over a road to reach the car park at the beginning of the walk.

You reach a stile and come onto the roadway going through Peper Harow **H**.

▶ Continue ahead on the roadway, immediately passing a duck pond on your right and a church on your left. Later go through a wooden gate bearing right and steadily uphill. Ignore a footpath sign on your left and, when your track bears left towards a road, leave it to continue straight ahead towards a stile. Cross the road to the turning opposite

(signposted to Shackleford) and continue along the road for about ½ mile (800 metres). The Cyder House Inn (another possibility for a pub stop) is passed on your right and you reach a road junction in Shackleford **J**.

▶ Turn right on the road signposted to Godalming for about 150 yards (135 metres) where you then turn left down Rokers Lane. After passing some houses, a large field comes into view on your left.

▶ One of the Eashing Bridges that span the River Wey. Dating from the 13th century, the bridges were soundly constructed to withstand erosion by the river: the fact that they still survive to serve their original purpose is evidence of their builders' skill.

JOHN GLOVER

now a Surrey County Council special school, was built in 1775, on the site of the original. As you walk up the lane, notice the 17th-century granary through the gateway on the right. It was raised on stilts to prevent attack by rodents.

In the village of Shackleford **J**, there are some fascinating old cottages in the vicinity of the village shop and one has a serpentine wall similar to those usually found in Suffolk.

A little further along the walk are some steps **K** that were built by volunteers from one of the county's leading rambling groups, the Surrey County Walkers, as a contribution to

▲*The shorter version of the walk leads first along a bridleway, then along a path through woods.*

countryside conservation. This once quite treacherous path can now be used all year.

CANAL LINKS

Canoeists are the only ones easily able to negotiate the River Wey **L** at this point. The navigable portion, which is known as the Godalming Navigation, was built two centuries ago as a canal. It runs from the Town Bridge for 4½ miles (7.2 km) to Guildford. Here it joins the Wey Navigation and continues for another 14½ miles (23 km) to link with the Thames at Weybridge. The canal's entire length is in the care of the National Trust.

On the approach to Godalming, Boarden Bridge **M** crosses the River Wey. This low brick structure is well over 200 years old, and is the town's oldest surviving bridge.

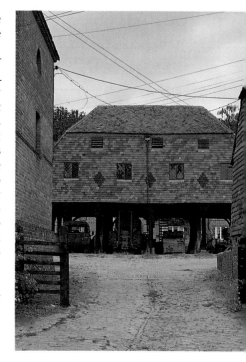

▲*The granary at Peper Harow was ingeniously built on stilts to deter rats and mice. The plaque (below) commemorates John George Phillips, a Godalming hero, who went down with the* Titanic.

Peace and Prosperity

'Let there be light, electric light', the residents cried, and in 1881 Godalming became the first town in the entire world to have its street lighting electrified. This truly fascinating and attractive town has produced many famous sons and its recorded history goes back even further than the time when Caesar's legions invaded these shores.

Just like Guildford, only 4½ miles (7.2 km) down the River Wey, Godalming had, by the mid-1500s, become one of the most productive cloth towns. For centuries it has benefited from having the essential ingredients of a healthy wool trade. There has always been a plentiful supply of water for washing the wool and driving the machinery, and this same water has provided the rich pastures on which sheep grazed.

Being a convenient staging post along the busy Portsmouth Road from London also contributed to the town's prosperity, as did other important industries of the past, including tanning, leather-working and paper-making. Even after the building of a by-pass in the 1930s, the growing vehicle ownership gradually turned the town centre into a driver's nightmare. A very recent road development has now re-routed the traffic, and the town centre has once again regained its former charm and tranquillity.

This handsome 'pepper pot' building is Godalming's former town hall, an outward sign of the town's prosperity.

The Cloister **N** is dedicated to the memory of John George (or Jack) Phillips. When the *Titanic* hit an iceberg on its maiden voyage in 1912, Jack Phillips, from neighbouring Farncombe, stayed at his post as chief wireless operator and sent distress signals until he, too, succumbed to his fate in the icy depths of the Atlantic Ocean.

An ancient church and downland views on London's outskirts

This walk through beautiful Surrey downland begins at Chaldon Church **Ⓐ**, which contains one of England's treasures. On the west wall is a mural, measuring 17 feet (5.2m) by 11 feet (3.3m). Dating from the 12th century, it is the earliest known English wall painting.

The picture is divided into two parts. The upper part shows men and women being welcomed by angels into heaven, and the lower one depicts large, evil-looking devils punishing the wicked. The artist, supposedly a travelling monk, displays all the best qualities of the medieval mind — humour, liveliness and a deep, sincere piety.

The pulpit, dated 1657, is one of very few to have been erected

▶ *This sign commemorating Chaldon's 900th anniversary is on the small green near the 12th-century church.*

during the rule of Oliver Cromwell, and the ancient font, carved out of a single block of local stone, is also remarkable; the tool marks of the medieval masons are clearly visible. From the church, you walk across the aptly named Happy Valley, towards Old Coulsdon.

THE PRIEST'S WOODS

West of Old Coulsdon, you pass a wooded area, Parson's Pightle **Ⓑ**, the land allocated by Saxon law to the resident priest. Woodlands **Ⓒ** further on show signs of careful management in the past, with many coppiced hazels. The hazels were

▲*Happy Valley runs along below the wooded slopes of Farthing Down. The dark green fritillary (inset) is one of the butterflies that may be seen here. It can be spotted flying in June and July.*

FACT FILE

✳ Chaldon Church and Happy Valley, 2 miles (3.2km) west of Caterham

🆗 Pathfinder 1207 (TQ 25/35), grid reference TQ 308556

miles 0 1 2 3 4 5 6 7 8 9 10 miles
kms 0 1 2 3 4 5 6 7 8 9 10 11 12 13 14 15 kms

◔ Allow a minimum of 2 hours

◗ Generally easy but two short, stiff climbs. Strong shoes are advisable as the chalk is flinty and can be slippery

🅿 Good parking area in front of Chaldon Church

🍺🍴 None on the route but all facilities are in Chaldon village,
🚻 ½ mile (800m) south of the church

THE WALK

CHALDON CHURCH – HAPPY VALLEY

The walk begins at Chaldon Church **Ⓐ**. Take the B2031 and follow signs for the church, north-west of Chaldon village.

▶ With the church on your left, walk back past the green to the lane. Turn left and, a few paces along the lane, turn right on the footpath signposted 'Happy Valley'. Follow the path ahead as it bears half left up the field towards a gap in the line of woods that you can see on the skyline.

▶ At the top of the rise the path runs just to the right of the woods. It then continues straight ahead over the field and down the slope on the other side towards more woods.

▶ Keep straight on through the wood. You come out of the trees on a grassy hillside looking down on Happy Valley. Keep straight on down the hill with a hedge on your right-hand side.

▶ Cross over a gravel track and take the narrow path climbing steeply through woods.

▶ As you leave the woods you will see a signpost. Bear right, following the sign for Coulsdon Common. As you reach the top of the rise the track becomes wider and you may prefer to follow a parallel path through trees on the left. Follow the track until you come to a parking area and a footpath to the left signed 'Old Coulsdon'. Follow the footpath to the road and bear left along the footpath beside it. On your left is a wooded area, Parson's Pightle **Ⓑ**.

▶ Turn left down Lacey Avenue. At the T-junction cross the road and turn right. Take the second turning to the left to go down a narrow lane signposted 'Bridle Road to Farthing Downs and Woodplace Lane'.

▶ Past Tollers Riding Stables, the lane becomes an attractive tree-shaded path. Keep on downhill until you come to a footpath sign at a fork. Bear right on a bridleway marked 'Woodplace Lane/ Farthing Downs'. The path plunges steeply downhill through interesting woodland **Ⓒ**. Keep straight on over a junction of paths. Climb through the trees ahead up a series of broad wooden steps.

▶ Just before you reach the top you come to a crossing track. Turn left, under a barrier, to come out on the open hillside of Farthing Downs **Ⓓ**. The route is along the top of the Downs. Do not follow the more obvious path, signed with a yellow waymark arrow, that runs downhill, but keep right of a picnic bench along the top of the hill. Follow this path as it joins a wider way, bears a little more to the left and leads through Devilsden Wood **Ⓔ** towards Happy Valley. At a fork, bear left.

▶ At the end of the woods are grass covered slopes and a signpost indicating a permissive footpath straight on to Chaldon Church. Follow this, with the woods close on your right, until you come to the path taken earlier, signposted 'Chaldon Church'. Turn right along the path back to the start of the walk.

PHILIP CRAVEN

regularly cut down almost to ground level, so that they would produce a crop of vigorous young shoots that could be cut for building and fencing. The sharp-eyed may also spot badger setts here.

ALONG THE DOWNS

The route skirts Old Coulsdon and returns to the Downs. The ground is hard chalk with flints and is mostly unfarmed. A great variety of downland wild flowers — lovers of chalk soil — can be found in the area.

Farthing or Fairdean Downs **Ⓓ**

◀ *The 'Trim Trail', just off the route south of Old Coulsdon, is a half-mile (800m) circuit with twelve exercises.*

are crossed by a very old route marked by Bronze Age tumuli. Further north, there is an extensive Celtic rectangular field system.

From the heights, there is a beautiful view of Happy Valley and there are some good spots at which to stop for a picnic. The route continues along the side of the valley through Devilsden Wood **Ⓔ** — literally 'the dark place'. With its sombre glades of yew, it lives up to its name. Adding contrast are tall beeches and oaks and very large hawthorns. Wild clematis drapes the downland bushes, and the paths are bordered with wild mint. After exploring Happy Valley, you rejoin the path back to the church.

Around a beauty spot on the borders of West Sussex and Hampshire

▲ *The tree-clad western slopes of the Devil's Punch Bowl are the summer home of the nightjar (inset), usually seen in flight at dusk but rarely during the day, when it roosts on the ground.*

The Devil's Punch Bowl is in the Greensand, the area between the chalk of the Downs and the clays of the Weald. Here, soft sandstone has been eroded away by numerous springs to create a spectacular, steep-sided depression that is now in the care of the National Trust.

The western slopes are covered in pine trees, but the other sides remain bracken-covered and bleak. On these steep slopes and in the bottom of the basin, Victorian naturalists identified several rare ferns; including the flowering fern, sweet mountain fern and marsh fern. The area is also rich in wild flowers. Look for bog pimpernel, sundew and guelder rose, among others.

TREE-CLAD SLOPES

The walk starts from a National Trust car park by the crossroads village of Hindhead, on the high ground above the Punch Bowl. The route follows the edge of the tree-clad western slopes. At first, the

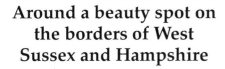

FACT FILE

- ✳ Hindhead, 2 miles (3.2km) north of Haslemere

- ▱ Pathfinder 1245 (SU 83/93), grid reference SU 890357

  miles 0 1 2 3 4 5 6 7 8 9 10 miles
  kms 0 1 2 3 4 5 6 7 8 9 10 11 12 13 14 15 kms

- ◓ 1¾ hours

- ◣ One steep ascent and descent

- Ⓟ National Trust car park on north side of A3, 200 yards (180m) east of the junction with the A287

- ⍟ Refreshments available in Hindhead and Haslemere

trees screen the bowl below, but soon a steep downward path goes through the trees, and long views begin to open up. The air becomes more still as you descend; the deeper you go, the quieter it gets.

RARE FERNS

Almost at the bottom, a turn along a bridleway is followed by another path which goes down to a stream Ⓐ. It is along the sandy banks of this musical little brook that you will find the ferns sought out by the Victorian naturalists. The springs around here have so cut into the sandy soil that the valley floor is narrow and you begin to climb again, through a thin screen of trees, as soon as you cross the water.

Very soon, the path enters a beautiful glade. Ahead is the Hindhead Youth Hostel Ⓑ, made up of three cottages that were once the homes of broom makers. Their craft was once, literally, a cottage industry here.

From the hostel, you follow a

THE WALK

HINDHEAD – GIBBET HILL

The walk begins at the National Trust car park on the A3.

1 Take the path into the woods immediately behind the Hillcrest Café. Turn left along the first crossing path and follow this for about ¼ mile (400m). At a junction of paths, follow the blue waymark arrow, and, soon after, fork right on a path going steeply downhill. Turn left on a crossing track at the bottom and, in 50 yards (45m), turn right along a downhill path, with a wire fence on the left, until you reach a stream **A**.

2 Cross the plank bridge, and continue uphill on the path ahead to a grassy clearing in front of Hindhead Youth Hostel **B**. Turn left on a clear path,

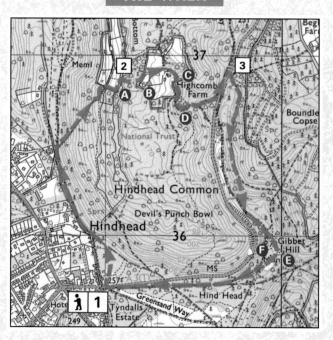

then bear right along a gravel track uphill, through a gate and ahead past Highcombe Farm **C**. The track becomes a narrow road. Follow this uphill.

There is a viewpoint **D** just off the road when it bends sharp left. Shortly after, bear left on a bridleway waymarked with a red arrow, and follow it to

come to the A3.

3 Cross this busy road with care to a footpath opposite, signposted to Hindhead Common. The path immediately forks. Keep right uphill, following the sunken path for ¼ mile (400m) to another fork. Again, go right and uphill to join a bridleway. Turn left. When it splits into three, take the middle track and, after a few paces, turn right between wooden posts and follow a path running uphill. Pass a large stone cross and an open viewpoint at Gibbet Hill **E**. Head for an earth-banked enclosure, and bear right along a narrow byway. The monument stone **F** is on the right in 100 yards (90m). Continue on this road until it converges with the A3, opposite the car park at the start.

---

wider track past the picturesque half-timbered buildings of High-combe Farm **C** on to a tree-lined road. At a bend, it is worth taking the path through the bracken for a few yards to get a wonderful overview of the Punch Bowl **D**. A little further along the road, a bridle path to the left gives further long vistas to the north over the Weald.

You cross the busy Portsmouth road to another path, which climbs gently along an old sunken boundary to level ground again. You are now on the eastern rim of the depression. You follow this as it curls left to Gibbet Hill **E**. The summit, 892 feet (272m) high, is short-grassed and bare of trees, and offers good views over the Weald.

GIBBET HILL

The hill was named after an incident in 1786, when the bodies of three men, executed for the brutal murder of an unknown sailor, were hung here in chains. The men, also sailors, had met their young victim at the Red Lion in Thursley, and offered to travel with him to Portsmouth. Near this spot, they killed him, stole his clothes and money, and hurled his body down the slope. The deed was soon discovered, and the murderers were arrested later that day at the

BOTH PHOTOS: DEREK FORSS

◀ *The approach to Gibbet Hill is via an old sunken land boundary which climbs gently to the summit of the hill.*

▲ *From the summit of Gibbet Hill, where murderers' bodies once hung, there are fine views over the Weald.*

Flying Bull at Rake. Shortly after leaving Gibbet Hill, you pass a memorial stone **F** to their victim. It was erected in 1786 by James Stilwell of Cosford 'in the detestation of the barbarous murder committed here on an unknown sailor'.

This stone stands beside a quiet lane that turns just south of the current course of the A3 and returns you to the start of the walk.

SURREY

◄*Parts of Cudworth Manor, whose moat is topped up by a nearby brook, are 13th-century. The wild service tree (inset), pictured here in autumn, is an unusual species seen in Glover's Wood.*

Lovely, peaceful countryside just a mile from Gatwick's runways

Charlwood is a large village set in green farmland. The walk begins at its picturesque heart — an attractive group of cottages by the Half Moon Inn, close to the golden sandstone Church of St Nicholas **Ⓐ**. The church has a beautifully carved and painted 15th-century chancel screen, recently restored to its original brilliance. The 13th-century wall paintings, revealed under white-wash in 1858, were restored in 1962.

The path from the village provides two surprises; the sight of old military helicopters and aircraft awaiting restoration, and the sounds of exotic creatures from Gatwick Zoo **Ⓑ**, which is away to the left.

The ancient Glover's Wood **Ⓒ** is deliciously cool and refreshing on a hot day, and contains some unusual species, such as wych elm, small-leaved lime and wild service tree.

The route follows country lanes and a sweeping drive to Home Farm **Ⓓ**, which was once a wing of 16th-century Newdigate Place. Parts of the timber-framed quadrangle are visible in the farm buildings.

The finest house in the scattered hamlet of Cudworth is Cudworth Manor **Ⓔ**. Part dates from the 13th century. It is surrounded by a broad moat fed by a brook, and crossed by an attractive roofed bridge.

You return to Charlwood on quiet lanes. Views of the North Downs from Beggarshouse Lane include Box Hill, perhaps the best-known beauty spot in Surrey.

Tucked away in Charlwood are several exquisite timber-framed and tile-hung cottages. Bristows, or School Cottage **Ⓕ**, was built about 1620 as a charity school for boys and remained one for 250 years, while Laurel Cottage is a small 'open hall' cottage, built to a medieval plan. The houseleeks on the low roof to the right of Tudor Cottage were encouraged by country people, who believed they offered protection against witchcraft and fire.

GALLETED MUSEUM

The stone 'Cage' **Ⓖ**, now a small museum, was once the village lock-up. The use of small pieces of black ironstone to decorate the uneven mortar joints is a typical Surrey feature, known as 'galleting'.

Providence Chapel **Ⓗ** looks like something from the set of a Wild West film. It came from Horsham, where troops guarding the coast against a possible Napoleonic invasion had used it as a guardroom.

The last part of the walk follows Black Ditch, an old causeway made of local paludina limestone, which is too hard to cut as free-stone, but is a perfect material for paving.

▼*The ponds of Green Lane Farm Fishery attract wildfowl and anglers.*

FACT FILE

☀	Charlwood, 3 miles (4.8km) north of Crawley
◱	Pathfinder 1227 (TQ 24/34), grid reference TQ 241410

miles 0 1 2 3 4 5 6 7 8 9 10 miles
kms 0 1 2 3 4 5 6 7 8 9 10 11 12 13 14 15 kms

◔	3 hours
▭	Mostly level walking. Field and woodland paths may be muddy and overgrown. Wear good walking shoes and trousers
Ⓟ	On side streets in Charlwood
🍺	Rising Sun and Half Moon, both in Charlwood
WC	Behind pavilion on recreation ground
♜	Gatwick Zoo is open Mar–Oct, daily, 10.30am–6pm; winter weekends and school holidays, 10.30am–4pm. Admission charge. Tel. (01293) 862312

THE WALK

CHARLWOOD – CUDWORTH

Begin at the Half Moon pub in Charlwood.

1 Facing the pub, turn right towards the church **A**. Follow the paved path left through the churchyard to the lych-gate. Continue on the paved path out of the churchyard and past a field on the left to a road.

2 Cross and walk down Glover's Road opposite. At the end, continue on the private road signposted to the Woodland Trust and Little Glover's Farm. At the end, cross a stile and follow a fenced path towards woods. Gatwick Zoo **B** is visible to the left.

3 Go through a kissing-gate into Glover's Wood **C**. Continue straight ahead through the wood. Descend to cross a footbridge then continue uphill in the same direction.

Cross a semi-paved ride onto the waymarked path opposite. Follow it to the edge of the wood.

4 Turn left to follow a bridlepath, just inside the wood's boundary, to a road. Turn right and walk to the junction. Go right along Partridge Lane, take the first left (Duke's Road), and continue ahead between two lakes, through a gate and along Duke's Drive to Home Farm **D**. As the lane bends left opposite the farm, a waymarked metal gate to the right leads to a bridleway, which soon goes through another metal gate into a long pasture. Make for the gate and stile ahead.

5 Climb the stile, and strike out diagonally right across the field. Aim for the rustic bridge between two lakes. Cross and take the first gate right. Walk beside the lake to a

footbridge in the trees, and go through the waymarked gate. The footpath goes diagonally across the next field (it may be easier to keep to the left-hand edge, past the deer farm) to the stile in the far corner.

6 Cross the next short field, keeping left, and look carefully for the next stile, which is rather overgrown. The footpath continues along the unfenced edge of the garden of Darragh House, and on to the lane by the house's driveway. Turn left to the junction. Cudworth Manor **E** is a short way to the left. Turn right past the manor farm. Follow the lane to the road by Holly Farm.

7 Climb the stile opposite and go diagonally right to a gateway in the far corner. Turn left on the footpath along the right-hand edge of the next two fields. Enter a small wood, and climb a stile on the right. Turn left along Beggarshouse Lane to the main road. Turn right (a path in the trees on the right saves walking against traffic). Cross the lane leading to Barfield Farm, to

a stile in the wood.

8 Cross and go through the field, keeping left. Enter a wood left of a large hollow, climb a stile at the end and go ahead through two fields to the road. Turn left past School Cottage **F** and Laurel Cottage. At the junction, cross, turn right and walk past Elm Cottage, set back just after the Post Office.

9 Turn left up the lane just after the Rising Sun. Pass the Cage **G** on the right, and take the next right past Tudor and Old Rosemary Cottages. At the end, turn left to see Mores and Swan Cottages, then return past the school and go left on an unmade road to Providence Chapel **H**. Return along the unmade road and go ahead down Chapel Road. Just before the T-junction, take a path left between two hedges. Cross the road to see the Old Mill, set well back. Turn right and walk diagonally left across the recreation ground. Cross the road and take the paved footpath opposite, between high hedges, to the Half Moon.

A stroll through William the Conqueror's hunting grounds

This walk reveals the peaceful beauty of the New Forest at its most charming. It follows tracks in mixed oak and beech woodland for which the forest is famous.

These woods are the home of many wild creatures, including badgers and fallow deer. Less shy are the ponies with their leggy foals and the squirrels leaping from branch to branch overhead. Dead trees and ant hills are the favourite haunt of woodpeckers — all three of our native species are here. Many rare species of plants flourish in the oak woods, including orchids and the wild gladiolus.

Churchplace Cottage **Ⓐ** is one of the original New Forest Keepers' cottages. A charming brick cottage, it was built in 1810 when the Forest

The mixed woodlands of the New Forest are a perfect habitat for birds including the green woodpecker (inset).

was divided into 'walks' and a Keeper appointed for each walk. All the cottages had an orchard and a paddock. Nowadays, a Keeper's duties are more varied.

In 1079 William the Conqueror declared west of Southampton Water to the Avon valley and north of the Solent to the Wiltshire Downs his personal hunting forest. The Saxon chroniclers, who hated the Norman king, wrote that in

doing so, he destroyed many Saxon villages. They claimed he also destroyed their churches, a much worse crime since this was sacrilege. Church Place **Ⓑ** is the name of a knoll which has survived the centuries and occurs on old maps. This suggests that it could have been the site of a destroyed church and perhaps a village. Follow the track on to the knoll and you will discover

FACT FILE

* Ashurst, on the eastern boundary of the New Forest, 7 miles (11km) west of Southampton on A35

* Outdoor Leisure Map 22, grid reference SU 335103

  miles 0 1 2 3 4 5 6 7 8 9 10 miles
  kms 0 1 2 3 4 5 6 7 8 9 10 11 12 13 14 15 kms

* Allow 1 hour

* Very easy, ideal for families with young children. Perfect for an evening stroll when there is a better chance of seeing the shyer animals

* **P** In Ashurst village

* Shops, pubs and restaurants in Ashurst village, also takeaways. New Forest Hotel has children's playground

* **T** Trains from Southampton and Bournemouth (alight at Lyndhurst Road). Two bus services available

Delightful Churchplace Cottage is home to one of the New Forest Keepers.

BOB GIBBONS. INSET. HUGH CLARK/NATURE PHOTOGRAPHERS

BOB GIBBONS

THE WALK

ASHURST - CHURCHPLACE INCLOSURE

The walk begins in the car park in Ashurst village, close to the A35 Southampton-Bournemouth road .

1 Leave the car park on the east side, immediately crossing the hospital access road. The hospital, a large white building formerly the New Forest Union workhouse, is on your right as you bear right down a wide tarmac track which shortly changes to gravel. Continue past the Forestry Commission barrier. The village cricket ground is now on your right. Follow the track towards Churchplace Inclosure woods which you will see lying ahead.

2 Just before you reach the woods the track turns right beside Churchplace Cottage **Ⓐ** . Follow the track right, through the gate and on into the lovely mixed woodlands. Keep to the gravel track, ignoring

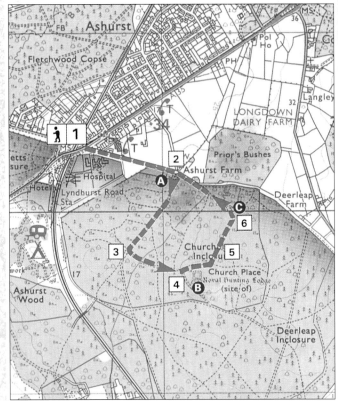

all green crossing paths.

3 After about ³/4 mile (1.2km), another gravel track joins on the left. Turn left along this. Keep to the gravel path past two green joining paths on the left.

The track rises slightly ahead and you will see it turning to the right at the top of the rise.

4 Turn left along the green path leading from the corner of the right

bend in the gravel track. The green path leads round a knoll on your right crowned with tall beech trees. This is Church Place **Ⓑ**, possibly the site of a Saxon village. Continue along this pretty path under the sweet chestnut trees as it bears to the left.

5 The small path meets a much broader green way joining on the right. Do not turn right, but continue straight on.

6 The path divides in front of a wooden seat. Turn left here to follow a raised tree-shaded path downhill, close to the Forest border. An interesting, low-lying area **Ⓒ** is on your right. Keep straight on past all joining tracks until you see Churchplace Cottage again in front of you. Turn right through the gate, then left to follow the gravel track back to the car park in Ashurst.

some intriguing embankments and ditches. The remains of the hunting lodge later built here could well have been built on top of the old foundations.

The green path which leads round the knoll has turf like a smooth lawn, cropped short by the New Forest ponies. The ponies' action preserves the green lawns and rides of the beautiful New Forest. They could be called the first conservationists!

There is a strange, low-lying area to the right of the path containing deep pits **Ⓒ**. This could have been caused by the practice of digging marl. Marling — digging for material in the forest which could be spread to improve the quality of the soil — is still one of the New Forest Commoners' ancient rights. Others include gathering fuel and pastur-

ing animals. These were the Saxon forest dwellers' rights which survived the Norman conquest and are still jealously guarded by the Commoners of the New Forest today, hundreds of years later.

▲ *In early times ponies roamed all over Britain, but as farming and the population increased they were contained in small areas including the New Forest. Herds of ponies have been in this area since Saxon times.*

A FOREST ARBORETUM

◀ *Woodland of the Forest includes birch, pine, sweet chestnut and old woods of beech and oak. The oak woods are favoured by fallow deer (inset). Late June is a good time to spot fawn.*

To reach the starting point for the walk you turn off one of the New Forest's most famous avenues, Rhinefield Ornamental Drive **A**.

RARE CONIFERS

This was originally a track leading to a forest lodge, with grounds used as a tree nursery by earlier foresters. In 1859 the drive was planted as an avenue of rare and mainly imported conifers, shrubs and rhododendrons. Now some of these trees are among the tallest in Britain and include statuesque giant redwoods and Douglas firs. The Wellingtonia redwood species boasts the tallest tree in the world, which grows in California. The Wellingtonias in the New Forest will grow only half the

BOB GIBBONS. INSET: R. FLETCHER/SWIFT PICTURE LIBRARY

A New Forest walk among rare and magnificent trees

This walk is a fairly flat meander among some of the most beautiful trees of the New Forest. The woods of this southern part of the Forest are among its most outstanding. They include ancient trees that have been standing for over two and three hundred years of the forest's 900-year history.

Oak, beech, yew and holly are among the oldest trees. The poor soil of the New Forest stunts the size of trees and shortens life. However, in spite of this disadvantage, some of the oaks, which are the oldest of the trees, can be up to 400 years of age — so they were young saplings at the time of Queen Elizabeth 1. The forest also contains some of the tallest conifers in Britain.

FACT FILE

- ⚲ Rhinefield Ornamental Drive, Brockenhurst, 3 miles (4.8 km) west of Lyndhurst off the A35 Christchurch-Southampton road

- 🗺 Outdoor Leisure Map 22, grid reference SU 267047

  miles 0 1 2 3 4 5 6 7 8 9 10 miles
  kms 0 1 2 3 4 5 6 7 8 9 10 11 12 13 14 15 kms

- 🕐 Allow 2½ hours

- ▬ Easy walk along mainly wide gravel tracks. Waterproof footwear is necessary in very wet weather

- P Blackwater car park, Rhinefield Drive. (Has picnic tables and benches)

- 🍴 Rhinefield House Hotel offers snacks and cream teas

- WC Blackwater car park

- I New Forest Museum in the car park at Lyndhurst is open from 10am to 5pm every day, except for Christmas Day

THE WALK

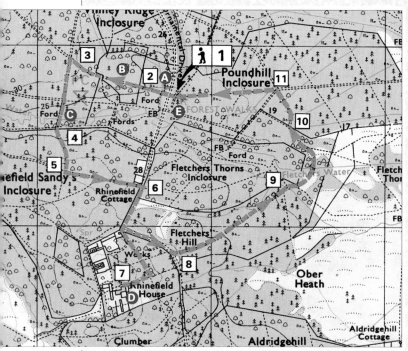

RHINEFIELD DRIVE – RHINEFIELD HOUSE – POUNDHILL ENCLOSURE

The walk starts at Blackwater car park on the Rhinefield Ornamental Drive.

1 Return to the entrance of the car park and go straight across the Rhinefield Ornamental Drive **A** and up the gravel drive opposite, passing round a low single-bar gate. Ahead of you is the Blackwater Arboretum **B**.

2 Go through the kissing gate into the arboretum and keep to the gravel drive that continues through the centre of it, then out of the gate at the far end. A fence designed to keep out the forest deer surrounds the arboretum.

3 Continue straight on and, at the first intersection in the gravel track, turn left. Follow this gravel drive down an incline, across another wide gravel path and straight on down to the Black Water River **C**. The track crosses the river by a concrete platform that is usually dry because the water is channelled through pipes below.

4 The track snakes to the left, then to the right, up a slope. The woods on either side of you are home to fallow and, less commonly seen, red and roe deer. Conifers are to the right of you, deciduous woodland on the left.

5 When you reach a T-junction with another gravel track, and a grass ride leads off straight ahead, turn left. Follow this gravel track until you reach workshops, then a forest cottage on the right and come back to Rhinefield Drive.

6 Turn right onto the tarmac road and follow this for a short distance. Where the road turns sharp left, go straight ahead up the drive to Rhinefield House **D**.

7 Leave the house by the same drive and turn right on to Rhinefield Drive at the end. Continue along the road for a short distance until you reach a gravel track on the left. Turn down this track.

8 Rhododendrons and other evergreen shrubs line the track at first then, on the right-hand side, an area of young conifers can be seen. Look out for the narrow deer paths on either side. Continue along this track for some distance. There are no intersections.

9 Ignore a grass ride that eventually leads off on your left and continue along the gravel track that bears, in snake-like curves, first to the right and then to the left through hemlocks, the familiar Christmas-tree spruces. The track then crosses the river by a concrete ford that can become covered by shallow water in extremely wet weather.

10 At the Y-junction, take the fork to the right. Soon after this, the gravel track is crossed by a second gravel track.

11 At this junction a grass ride goes off diagonally to the left. Take this grass ride, continue straight ahead when a second grass ride cuts across it and you will find yourself back in the car park. From here you can take a further excursion along the Forestry Commission's waymarked walk **E**.

height of the native Californian species, but they still outstrip most other species in this country.

The start of the walk takes you through an arboretum planted a century later, in 1959 and 1960. The Blackwater Arboretum **B** contains some special young trees all labelled with their species, including dragon spruce and locust trees. These widely spaced youngsters appear midgets beside their older neighbours and all are carefully protected from the destructive deer by a 12-foot (3.6-metre) high fence.

Passing out of the arboretum, the wide gravel track leads down to the Black Water River **C**. This river gets its name from the brown hue of the water, which appears even darker as it runs under closely growing conifers that allow little light and a minimum of forest floor growth.

STORM DAMAGE

In World War II, this area received some of the first flying bombs, which caused many forest fires. Now there is little evidence of that destruction, except a few shallow pits, but everywhere there are signs of the great storms of 1987 and 1990.

The woods are home to many typical woodland birds — great and lesser spotted woodpeckers, nuthatch and tree creeper, as well as some that are more rare, such as the crossbill and hawfinch. Little owls can sometimes be seen in daylight in the summer breeding season when they are having to provide a supply of food for their young.

Fallow, red and the smaller roe deer are all to be found here. Fallow, with their slim and graceful outlines and spotted coats in summer, are the deer you are most likely to see. You may also spot a few of the much

◀An amelanchier shrub in flower, one of the young species planted in the Blackwater Arboretum that is passed through at the beginning of the walk.

▶The Black Water River, looking downstream, is one of many rivers running through the forest. These tributaries join to swell the Lymington River above Balmer Lawn Bridge.

rarer white fallow deer.

During the mating season of fallow and red deer in October, the early-morning and evening woods ring out with the roar of a red stag or a fallow male's bark, similar to a repeated and resonant pig snort!

VULNERABLE FAWNS

In May and June the fawns are born and remain hidden in the undergrowth while their mothers feed nearby. It is very important at this time of the year to keep dogs on the lead as these young animals are very vulnerable. Each year well-meaning people, especially children, find new-born fallow fawns and red deer calves, apparently abandoned. Usually a very anxious mother is watching from close by and they are much better left untouched.

Roe deer produce their kids from mid-April to mid-June and twins are not uncommon. Although roe mate much earlier than the other deer species, in late July to early August, the fertilized egg remains undeveloped until December.

MASTER KEEPER'S LODGE

Gravel drives lead you past a typical forest cottage and briefly back onto Rhinefield Drive, then up to Rhinefield House ❿ which is well worth a visit. This spot has an aristocratic history, being once the site of William the Conqueror's hunting lodge and also at a later date the site of a hunting lodge used by Charles II. The house now standing was built around 1890 by Nottinghamshire collieries' heiress, Mabel Walker, at the time of her marriage to Captain Lionel Munro. It stands, approximately, on the site of the original Master Keeper's lodge. (The Barber and Walker collieries were the inspiration for many of D H Lawrence's novels.)

The house was constructed and decorated in a mixture of styles that appealed to the couple. The mainly neo-Elizabethan exterior has chimneys copied from Hampton Court and each balcony represents a Shakespeare play.

RHINEFIELD DECOR

On their honeymoon the Walker-Munros travelled widely and came back with many interior design ideas. Mabel's bedroom copied a room in a chateau on the Loire and as a Christmas present she presented Lionel with a smoking room that took its design from the Alhambra Palace in Granada. Its exotic oriental style appears in wonderful rich peacock colours. The domed ceiling has a star in Venetian glass in the centre. The stained glass windows, covered in a filigree of lattice work, would have permitted the women enclosed in the harem a view of the

◀The land now occupied by Rhinefield House was originally the site of William the Conqueror's hunting lodge.

The New Forest Embroidery

Situated 3 miles (4.8 km) away, in the car park at Lyndhurst, is the New Forest Museum, which houses the New Forest embroidery. Nearly 25 feet (8 metres) long and over 2½ feet (75 cm) high, it is a wonderfully constructed and beautifully executed work of art that depicts not only the history and people of the Forest, but its beauty through the seasons and the wealth of birds, animals and flowers to which the area is home.

In 1979, when the New Forest reached its 9th century, the New Forest Association wanted to

King William and a Cistercian monk with a model of Beaulieu Abbey in the first panel.

establish a permanent record of the history of this unique area of Britain. An embroidery that showed its history and its moods was chosen as the best form of record. This embroidery was designed by someone who knows the forest well; Belinda Montagu lives in the forest and is a designer, teacher and lecturer in embroidery.

The background is mainly of silk taffeta and silk organza and these materials were first applied to the canvas. Then the tree trunks and foliage were attached. Finally, the multitude of birds, animals and flowers were included in the foreground. Local volunteers made up the smaller symbols — animals, birds, tree trunks and heraldic devices — from kits sent to them that included the canvas with the design outlined and the materials.

The figures that appear throughout the embroidery were all worked by Belinda Montagu for continuity. They show the many well-known people involved with the area, including at the end, the Queen planting an oak sapling in 1979 to commemorate the 900th anniversary of the forest. Camping is depicted together with the well-known view of Fawley oil refinery which dominates the skyline.

▲*This wooded path is bordered by a ditch that leads off Rhinefield Drive and is interspersed with deer tracks.*

On leaving Rhinefield House the walk continues along a gravel track lined with rhododendrons and other shrubs. In early June the rhododendrons are in flower and add clouds of colour, appearing in shades from palest lilac to deep purple. Narrow tracks lead off the path to either side and in wet weather cloven-hoofed tracks are clearly visible, highlighting the fact that there are well-used deer routes in this area.

TALL TREES

Back in the car park, if you have energy left, a short extra excursion of 1½ miles (2.5 km) takes you along a Forestry Commission waymarked walk. Tall Trees walk ❸ gives you a chance to admire the noble conifers on either side of Rhinefield Drive without walking along the road. This walk leads from the north end of the car park next to the toilets. On the route you can see a short section of bank and fence built in the style used in 1700 when the first New Forest enclosure was created here to keep the commoners' stock from eating the growing trees.

▼*The formal gardens of Rhinefield House, with clipped yew hedges, contrasts with the surrounding wilderness.*

male-dominated world outside in the original. The walls are of burnished, beaten copper and the floor a richly-patterned mosaic.

The house, now a hotel and timeshare, stands in gardens that have been replanted in the original formal style. This included over 1 mile (1.6 km) of clipped yew hedges, a maze, croquet lawn and an outdoor theatre linked by corridors of paths and canals.

LOCAL LANDMARK

Being built on a mound, the house has three vistas: to the south, east and to the west. The Forestry Commission, which is responsible for the trees of the forest, has to keep these vistas free of high-growing trees. This makes the house a useful landmark from many parts of the forest.

COASTAL MARSHES

26

BOB GIBBONS. INSET: G. HAKANSSON/FRANK LANE PICTURE AGENCY

Through a nature reserve by the sea — a year-long haven for birds

Flat but fascinating, these marshes include both salt and freshwater wetland that attracts birds from many parts of the world. Salt production was an important industry here for about 600 years. The area is of sufficient importance to make it part of a Site of Special Scientific Interest.

Almost as soon as you leave the car park you pass some of the ponds **Ⓐ** which make this area of such importance for bird conservation. At least 258 bird species have been recorded in the area. In summer the saltmarsh islands are used by breeding black-headed gulls, terns, oyster catchers, ringed plovers, redshanks and mallard. Many other species use the freshwater marshes.

In winter many birds that breed

FACT FILE

⚹ Pennington, Oxey and Keyhaven marshes, 2 miles (3.2 km) west of Lymington off the A337

🆗 Outdoor Leisure 22, grid reference SZ 318927

```
miles 0   1   2   3   4   5   6   7   8   9   10 miles
kms  0 1 2 3 4 5 6 7 8 9 10 11 12 13 14 15 kms
```

◗ Allow 4 hours

▭ East, flat walking. Waterproof footwear usually necessary. Coastal section very exposed in adverse weather

🅿 There is a small car parking area on Pennington Marshes where the walk starts. Car park also at Keyhaven

🍴 Refreshments at Chequers Inn, Lymington and the Gun Inn at Keyhaven

wc Keyhaven car park and at inns

▲*Keyhaven marshes were acquired in 1984 to add to existing coastal sites, creating an unspoilt area known for the richness of its bird life, including a rare winter visitor — a little gull (inset).*

in the far north come south to avoid the snow and extreme cold. Some that overwinter in this area are brent geese, shelduck, wigeon, teal, and sometimes goldeneye, long-tailed duck and shoveller.

SEA SALT

On this walk you will see signs of the dykes and salt pans **Ⓓ** of an earlier salt industry. Salt was first produced here in the 12th century and the industry survived for 600 years. Seawater was drawn into trenches, then shallow ponds, called salt pans. It was left to evaporate until reduced to a strong saline solution. This was boiled so only the salt remained. By the 18th century there were 163 saltpans in use in the area and between 1724 and 1766

4,600 tons of salt were produced.

If you decide to take a break along the walk the 17th-century Chequers Inn **B** with real ale and excellent food is an ideal stopping point. Soon after you pass the office of the Lymington and Keyhaven Nature Reserve **C**. The reserve is run by Hampshire County Council who publish a booklet available for a small fee from the reserve office, Tel. (01590) 674656, or from the County Countryside and Community Department, Tel. (01962) 846034.

Part of the walk goes along the top of a newly built sea wall **E**. During the winter of 1989/90 Lymington was severely flooded and the old sea wall was breached in a number of places.

BOB GIBBONS

▶ *This wetland area with fresh and salt water marshes, lagoons and mudflats was once the site of a salt industry.*

THE WALK

PENNINGTON MARSHES – KEYHAVEN MARSHES – OXEY MARSH

The walk starts at Pennington on the marsh. At the Pennington roundabout, just out of Lymington on the A337 Lymington-New Milton road, take the first exit, unsignposted, coming from Lymington. Ignore the road immediately off this to the left and continue down Pennington Lane, which has a no-through-road sign. Follow this road across the marsh until you can go no further. There is a barrier across the road with car parking space to the left. Park here.

1 Start back up the tarmac road you drove down. There are a number of ponds **A** on your right, a good place to see birds. Fairly soon the road bears to the left. Just before a pond on the bend turn right down a narrow gravel path that runs between barbed wire fences.

2 Continue along the path until you reach a group of cottages. Here the path turns left and then joins a narrow tarmac country road.

3 If you require refreshments make a short detour by turning left and continuing along the road to the Chequers pub **B**.

Otherwise, at a house with an old barn on the right you will see a public footpath sign that points up the house drive. Take the drive, a right-of-way, and pass in front of the house. Then follow the gravel track that runs ahead with the barn on the right.

4 The track soon narrows to single person width. Continue along this, ignoring a footpath off to the right. When the path widens to a gravel track suitable for vehicles you pass Salterns Cottage, the reserve warden's office **C**.

5 Continue along the road for a short distance, pass a large house on the left, then just before the pond on the right turn right through a six-bar metal gate along a path that runs beside Eight Acre Pond. Here you overlook some of the old salt pans **D**. The shallow tidal waters of Oxey Lake ahead of you are ideal for spotting wading birds.

6 Walk straight ahead, along the top of the new sea wall **E**. Ignore the path along the wall to the left,

unless you want to extend your walk by following the sea wall into Lymington. You soon reach a sluice gate with a narrow bridge across the top. Take the bridge and follow the path around the water's edge. (If the sluice gate is open, you will have to follow the path that runs down one side of the estuary and up the other.)

7 Continue on the path along the shore edge, then on top of the sea wall. Sandbags pushed into the wall show where the sea has burst through.

8 Continue along the sea wall. If you want to take a short cut follow a wide stony path that runs in a direct line inland from the sea wall back to the car park. Otherwise follow the

path along the top of the wall, or on the land side of it. The path continues around the beach edge, following the side of the small yacht harbour.

9 When you reach the road at the back of the harbour, turn right onto it. This narrow road soon leads you through a gate, and back to where you parked your car.

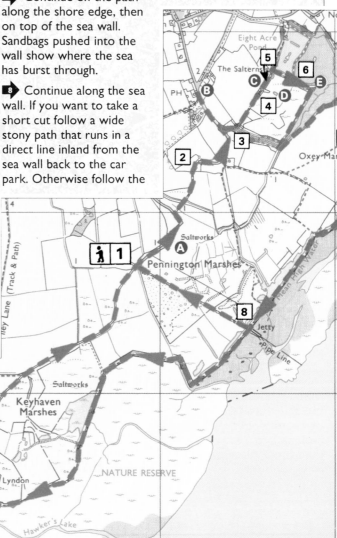

HIGH CORNER

27

HAMPSHIRE

A family stroll with safe paddling and forest lawns to picnic on

This is a delightful afternoon or summer evening stroll that offers complete freedom from traffic. You follow the course of Dockens Water, on the shallow river valleys that run west across the more remote northern areas of the New Forest to meet the River Avon. As you follow the streamside, the valley reveals all the gentle beauty and variety of New Forest scenery. Dark pinewoods contrast with the open glades of oak and beech that are home to roe and fallow deer, badgers and woodland birds including tree-creepers and woodpeckers. The path crosses the stream to climb the open hillside giving wide views of rolling woods and valleys.

A COACH INN

Here, where there are fewer people and no roads, there is a rich variety of heathland birds and plants. The white-washed High Corner Inn Ⓐ dates from the 1700s and was originally a farmhouse. During coaching days it thrived as an inn. Now this once-busy area of the Forest is the most quiet and remote and the Inn is well known for its excellent food. It also has a delightful woodland

BOB GIBBONS. INSET: AGENCE NATURE/NHPA

▲ *A quiet, shady spot in the New Forest at Woodford Bottom where Dockens Water runs through mixed woodland. The gudgeon (inset), a very small freshwater fish, swims in large shoals.*

garden overlooking the valley.

After a short walk through woodland you reach the stream known as Dockens Water Ⓑ. This stretch of water is associated with a New Forest heroine, Alice Lisle. She lived at Moyles Court, which is not far away, where the stream flows across the New Forest boundary. Although she was a staunch royalist — her husband was fighting for King James II — she sheltered two wounded fugitives, supporters of the Duke of Monmouth, who sought refuge in the Forest after his defeat at Sedgemoor. For this the gallant old lady was beheaded by order of the notorious Judge Jeffreys.

NO TRAITOR

Alice Lisle died standing, refusing to kneel and protesting she was no traitor. There is a memorial to her in the House of Commons.

Leaving the water over Splash Bridge, you arrive at Hasley Inclosure Ⓒ. There are lovely open views over the northern New Forest.

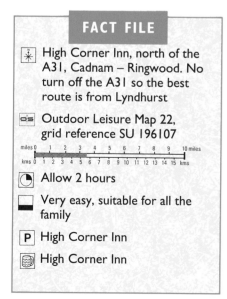

FACT FILE

- ☀ High Corner Inn, north of the A31, Cadnam – Ringwood. No turn off the A31 so the best route is from Lyndhurst

- ◧ Outdoor Leisure Map 22, grid reference SU 196107

  miles 0 1 2 3 4 5 6 7 8 9 10 miles
  kms 0 1 2 3 4 5 6 7 8 9 10 11 12 13 14 15 kms

- ◖ Allow 2 hours

- ▭ Very easy, suitable for all the family

- Ⓟ High Corner Inn

- ▦ High Corner Inn

THE WALK

HIGH CORNER – DOCKENS WATER

The walk begins at the High Corner Inn Ⓐ or the car parking area at Woodford Bottom close by. The High Corner Inn is north of the A31, Cadnam – Ringwood. You cannot turn off the A31 so the best route is from Lyndhurst. Follow the A35 through Lyndhurst towards Bournemouth. At Swan Green, just outside Lyndhurst, turn right for Emery Down. Drive through Emery Down and, just past the New Forest Inn, turn left along the road signposted to Bolderwood. Keep to this road as it bears north, under the A31, and follow it west over Broomy Plain. Turn right down the track signed 'High Corner Inn'. This track is gravel and has some potholes.

1 From High Corner Inn follow the track downhill. When it divides, turn right and walk the few paces to Woodford Bottom car park which is on your right. Follow the track straight ahead past the Forestry Commission car-free area barrier into the wood.

2 After about 100 yards (90 metres) you come to a gate. Do not go through the gate, but turn left towards Dockens Water Ⓑ with the Inclosure fence on your right. When you reach the streamside, turn right and follow the good path ahead with the Inclosure fence on your right and the stream on your left. Follow the streamside until you come to a cross track.

3 On your right the dark pine Inclosure gives way to young oak woods. On your left you will see a small curving concrete bridge (Splash Bridge). Turn left to cross the bridge, over Dockens Water. Follow the track ahead uphill as it curves a little left, then straightens to bring you uphill towards Hasley Inclosure Ⓒ.

4 When you are almost at the top of the hill you come to a crosstrack. Turn left here towards Hasley Inclosure.

5 Do not follow the main track through the gate into the Inclosure, but turn left just before the gate to walk along the hillside with the Inclosure fence on your right. (This path appears to run through the wood on the Ordnance Survey map but the trees have been felled here and you walk along open hillside.) When the path divides, keep straight on with the fence close on your right.

6 Keep to your path as it turns right to follow the Inclosure fence. Ahead, a little to your left, you will see a small rise crowned with a prominent group of pine trees. The path back to Dockens Water runs downhill just to the left of them. Follow the Inclosure fence until you are just past the pines on your left and you come to a cross track. On your right a track (barred) leads into Hasley Inclosure.

7 Turn left for just a few paces to meet the track to Dockens Water mentioned in Stage 6. Now turn right and follow the track downhill towards Dockens Water. (You will see High Corner Inn on the other side of the valley ahead of you.) As you come down into the valley you pass Ogden's Purlieu Ⓓ on your right.

8 Cross the small wooden footbridge over Dockens Water and walk up the gravel track ahead. When it divides you can turn left to your car at Woodford Bottom or keep straight on to walk up to High Corner Inn.

◄ *Splash Bridge crosses Dockens Water in the northern part of the New Forest, a wilder area than the busier south.*

Ogden's Purlieu Ⓓ, near the end of the walk, is a long, low building built around three sides of a square. The name 'purlieu' takes us back to the days of William the Conqueror. It is derived from the French *pour aller*, to walk round an area, and is the name given to land once subject to Forest laws but allowed to be enclosed and cultivated by special dispensation of the Crown.

The banks of the Inclosure, made soft by the roots of trees, are dotted with badger setts and their tracks can be seen leaving the trees and leading to the stream.

BOB GIBBONS

HAMPSHIRE

A walk round the well-preserved remains of a Roman town

There was a considerable settlement at Silchester before the Romans came. Eppilus, a tribal chief of the Atrebates, settled here in the 1st century AD, and traces of his town can be seen on this walk. The Roman name for the town, Calleva Atrebatum, means 'woody place of the Atrebates'. The Romans came later in the century, but the walls

▲*Near the start, the Roman walls curve around a delightful 12th-century church. Lesser reedmace (right), popularly known as the bulrush, grows in one of the ponds on the walk.*

FACT FILE

* Silchester, 6 miles (9.6km) south-west of Reading

▱ Pathfinder 1188 (SU 66/76), grid reference SU 643623

miles 0 1 2 3 4 5 6 7 8 9 10 miles
kms 0 1 2 3 4 5 6 7 8 9 10 11 12 13 14 15 kms

◖ Allow 2 hours

▬ Good walking on field paths and minor roads. Woods and valleys may be muddy

P By church at start

▤ Red Lion, Mortimer West End

I The Silchester excavations are accessible all year round. Blakes Lock Museum is open Tue–Fri 10am–5pm, Sat–Sun 2–5pm

◀*About halfway round the walk, the Red Lion at Mortimer West End is a convenient place for refreshments.*

visible today date from AD260-280.

The walls, 10 feet (3m) high in places, and 1½ miles (2.4km) in length, completely encircle the 100-acre (40-ha) site of the town. The town was laid out in a grid, with four gates, and contained baths, a forum and, later, a church. Just outside the walls is an amphitheatre.

When the Romans withdrew

from Britain at the beginning of the 5th century, the economy collapsed. The invading Anglo-Saxons were not town-dwellers, and urban life largely ceased in Britain until the 9th century. Then, many former Roman towns were reoccupied, and the remains pulled apart to provide building materials. The Roman buildings at Silchester, however, escaped largely intact, as the place remained mostly rural.

IMPRESSIVE CHURCH

The walk starts by the 12th-century Church of St Mary the Virgin Ⓐ, built just inside the wall, but outside the present town. Of particular interest inside are the lovely 14th-century tomb of Eleanor Baynard, a 17th-century pulpit and a 15th-century screen.

The route goes through the churchyard and past some Tudor farm buildings to join a track, The Drove, which runs through the middle of the Roman town to an earthen

THE WALK

SILCHESTER

*The walk begins at the car park by the Church of St Mary the Virgin **Ⓐ**, about 1 mile (1.6km) to the east of Silchester itself.*

1 Go through the churchyard to a kissing-gate. Bear right alongside a barn, and turn left through a gate to a straight track, The Drove. Follow this to a gap in the earth wall **Ⓑ**. Go left, with the embankment on your right, for 250 yards (225m), then turn right through a gap in the bank. Follow the track as it bears left, then goes straight on to a road by the Calleva Museum **Ⓒ**.

2 Turn right, and go straight on to a T-junction. Turn left towards Pamber Heath. After 400 yards (360m), turn right on the track just beyond Heatherbrae. Go straight ahead through the conifer plantation for 650 yards (600m). Just before going steeply downhill, turn right on a wide crossing track, which goes past the remains of an ancient fort **Ⓓ**. Follow the track out of the woods to a junction.

3 Bear left over the causeway between two ponds **Ⓔ**. On the other side, fork right and bear left uphill, then down to a valley. Cross a stream, then bear right and cross two more streams in quick succession before climbing uphill to a road.

4 Turn right. Pass the Red Lion and continue downhill, taking the bridleway that forks left by the stream. Follow this uphill to a road. Turn left. Follow this road as it bends right through some earthworks **Ⓕ**, and goes along Silchester's Roman Wall **Ⓖ** for 800 yards (720m). Where a lane joins the road at a sharp right bend, the amphitheatre **Ⓗ** is through a gate on your left. Follow the road round the bend to the start.

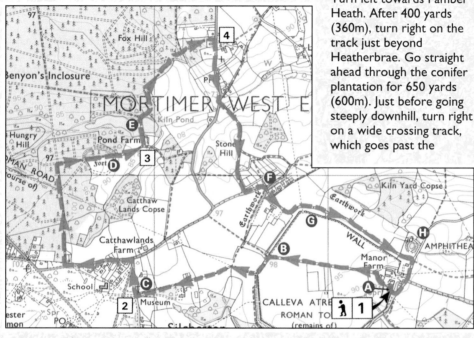

bank **Ⓑ** at the western end. If you climb the bank, you can see the size of the town and its encircling walls. In dry weather, it is possible to see the course of the old streets, picked out by the stunted or parched growth of the grass above them.

You follow the wall, then go between fields on a path alongside one of five Roman roads that radiated from Silchester. Look to the right at a five-bar gate across this path, and you can see the course of the road passing on a slight embankment over a ditch. You continue along a wider track to a road, where there is a museum.**Ⓒ** dedicated to the town.

PINE-CLAD HILLS

A short walk along the road takes you into a conifer plantation, then between two embankments that were once sections of a small fort **Ⓓ**. You come out of the woods into a delightful valley and cross a causeway between two ponds **Ⓔ**. The one on the left is large, and framed by gentle, pine-clad hills. Its smaller companion, covered with reeds and bulrushes, provides a habitat for abundant wildlife.

The route climbs up out of the valley onto a road where you will soon find a superb country pub, the Red Lion. It has a welcoming log fire in winter, and in summer you can sit in front of the flower-decked exterior and enjoy a view over low, rolling hills and streams.

A bridleway climbs one of these hills to a road, which passes through a gap in an earthwork **Ⓕ**, built by Eppilus, to follow the Roman Wall **Ⓖ**. This wall, with ironstone and limestone sandwiching courses of flint set in a mortar of gravel, sand and lime, is fronted by a ditch.

OVAL AMPHITHEATRE

At Manor Farm, a gate gives on to an oval amphitheatre **Ⓗ**, enclosed by high banks that would have had wooden seats sufficient for 4,000 people. From here, it is a short walk back past Manor Farm to the church, where the walk started. Beyond it, a well-preserved section of the wall, including the only survivor of the town's four gates, continues for some distance.

◄*Today, the Roman amphitheatre looks rather tame, but it was once the site of fierce gladiatorial combats.*

DEREK PRATT

The Wakes for most of his natural life. The work by which he is best remembered today, *The Natural History of Selborne*, was published in 1789, four years before his death, by his brother, a London bookseller.

A CLASSIC WORK

It was the first work addressing the subject of natural history to attain the status of an English classic, a status accorded it both because of its meticulous observations and its limpid prose style. The book was a composite of 110 letters to two friends and fellow naturalists, Thomas Pennant and Daines Barrington, and represented more than 20 years of work. The esteem in which it was, and still is, held led to the village becoming a magnet for amateur and professional naturalists from all over the world.

White is buried in a simple grave, inscribed 'G.W. 1793', on the north side of the chancel in the churchyard

◀*From Selborne Hanger there is an excellent view of the village below. Sweet woodruff (inset) grows well on the hangers' free-draining soil.*

A walk around the countryside studied by Gilbert White

Selborne sits on a spring line below a wooded hillside. The hills are of chalk, while the village itself is built on clays and malms. There are lovely thatched houses, but Selborne's most important building is The Wakes ④. Originally a small cottage built around 1500, it took its name from an early owner, who was probably a yeoman farmer.

In 1700, the building was purchased by Gilbert White, then vicar of Selborne, and was the home of his grandson and namesake, the famous amateur naturalist. It remained in the White family until 1844, and now houses two museums, one dedicated to the naturalist and the other to explorers Frank and Lawrence Oates (see box on page 4).

Gilbert White was born in Selborne, and lived and worked (as a clergyman like his grandfather) at

FACT FILE

⚹ Selborne, 4 miles (6.4km) south of Alton, on the B3006

🗺 Pathfinder 1244 (SU 63/73), grid reference SU 742335

miles 0 1 2 3 4 5 6 7 8 9 10 miles
kms 0 1 2 3 4 5 6 7 8 9 10 11 12 13 14 15 kms

◔ Allow 2½ hours

▬ Well defined paths and gentle slopes. Very muddy at times. Walking boots recommended

P Behind the Selborne Arms

T Infrequent bus service from BR stations at Alton and Petersfield

🏛 The Wakes, Tel. (01420) 511275 for opening times

I Hampshire Countryside and Community, Tel. (01962) 846045

THE WALK

SELBORNE – NOAR HILL

The route starts from The Selborne Arms.

1 Go north-west down the main street, passing The Wakes **A** on your left, and St Mary's Church **B** on your right. Turn left into Gracious Street. Follow the road past Grange Farm and Coneycroft House, with its lake lying at the foot of grassy banks. About 100 yards (90m) after the next right-hand bend, a shady bridleway goes off to your left.

2 Ascend on the bridleway, always keeping just inside the woods, with fields to your right. After 1 mile (1.6km) you descend gently, and keep ahead at a crossing of paths. At the edge of the wood, maintain your direction, then keep ahead along a track to a road.

3 Go through the gate opposite and diagonally left to the corner of the field. Turn right along a lane, then continue ahead up the bridleway when the lane bends left. Keep ahead over another lane, and continue along the edge of the field. Just before the top corner, turn left over a stile into the wood. You emerge at a crossing; keep ahead to join the Hangers Way, which comes up from the right after a few paces.

4 After 100 yards (90m) of gradual descent, fork left, still on the Hangers Way, onto the upper side of Noar Hill **C**. The path curls to the left, with good views, then descends on a rutted track, past the gated entrance to a nature reserve. Carry on out of the wood down the broad track to a road.

5 Turn right. At a junction beyond the thatched Lower Noar Hill Farm, go ahead over a stile, towards the woodland. At a fence, cross a stile on your left, leaving the Hangers Way, which turns right. Cross two more stiles into the wood and turn right, following a finger-post. After emerging into a field, bear left, keeping the hedgerow on your left, and exit through a tubular metal gate. At the end of a grassy path, you reach a drive. Turn left. (If you are pushed for time, turn right and follow this drive back to the start.)

6 Just past a junction where the Hangers Way comes in sharply from the right, take a footpath left up three stone steps. Walk between hedges to a gate giving access to National Trust land. Walk up the Bostal Path, turn left at the top and return down the zigzag **D** and back into Selborne and the start.

of St Mary's **B**, which is just across the road from The Wakes. The church dates from the end of the 12th century and is built in the Early English style. The huge yew in front — the trunk of which has been re-erected, after the January gales of 1990 claimed the tree — is of a similar age.

A stained glass window of St

◀ *St Mary's Church, built mainly of local flints, has changed little since Gilbert White's time as vicar.*

▲*The Wakes in Selborne, where Gilbert White lived, is now a museum to White and the Oates brothers.*

▲*There is much to explore around Selborne. Behind the church is Church Meadow (above) and just north-east of the village (off the route) are these cottages (below) at Short Lythe.*

Francis is dedicated to White's memory, and the whole airy interior of the church, which was sympathetically restored in the 19th century by Gilbert's nephew, William, is full of interesting details.

GRASSY SLOPES

Beyond the church, and well worth investigating if you have time, is the Glebe Field, or Church Meadow, whose grassy slopes lead to a steep-sided, wooded valley, where primrose, sweet violet, dog rose and wood spurge all flower abundantly in season.

The route leaves the village along a quiet country lane. Before long, you begin to climb, walking just inside the edge of the wooded Selborne Common, which is now owned by the National Trust. With the village of Newton Valence nearby to the east, the route climbs again to pick up the Hangers Way. This path, some 17 miles (27.2km) long, joins Alton in the north to Petersfield in the south.

THE HANGERS

The Way follows a series of steep-sided hills known in this part of East Hampshire as 'hangers', from the Old English 'hangra', or wooded slope. The route is waymarked by fingerposts and a distinctive logo depicting a tree on a hillside.

As you skirt Noar Hill ◉, there are some excellent views over the chalk downland to the south, and Woolmer Forest and the hills of Hindhead to the east. You pass some

Nature Walk

Beechwoods are home to many unusual plants, birds and other animals. Look out for these interesting wildlife features.

JUVENILE RING Beech trees with low branches retain a ring of dead leaves in winter, up to a height of approximately 8 feet (2.4m).

BADGER'S SETT Badgers like well-drained hillsides in which to build their homes, and the entrances to their setts are quite often found in hanger beechwoods.

WOODPECKER HOLE The green woodpecker, which is the largest resident woodpecker in Britain, excavates an oval nest hole, often quite high up the trunk.

BEECH TUFT FUNGUS Beechwoods are rich in fungi. This one grows on both living trees and dead wood.

▲ *The view from Selborne Common, looking back to the wooded Noar Hill.*

▶ *On a quiet, sunny evening on the village green it is easy to understand Gilbert White's love of the village.*

disused chalk pits, then cross farmland back to Selborne Common, climbing a little way in order to descend via the zigzag path **Ⓓ**.

This path was built in 1753 by Gilbert White and one of his brothers to give him easier access to the Common. There are delightful vistas through the beech trees that clothe the hanger, down to the village 200 feet (60m) below. At the bottom of the hill, you walk across a quiet green track back towards the starting point of the walk.

created it, that his spirit is most apparent. Just a ha-ha separates it from the green fields and the upward sweep of the hanger beyond. In the garden are a laburnum arch, a sundial White brought from Andover, and a brick path which he laid from the house to a wooden shelter he built for watching birds.

The gardens (left) at the rear of The Wakes, where Gilbert White no doubt mused on his sermons and on the natural history around him. The Wakes Museum houses mementoes of Captain Lawrence Oates, seen below with two of his ponies.

The Wakes Museum

In 1954, a Mr R W Oates purchased The Wakes. He made funds available to dedicate it as a memorial to Gilbert White, and to house memorabilia relating to Mr Oates's family, and specifically to his cousins, Frank and Lawrence Oates.

Frank Oates was born in 1840. A respected naturalist, he was a fellow of the Royal Geographical Society. In 1874, he realized his lifetime ambition of travelling to Africa to visit the Victoria Falls, but died of fever on his return journey.

Lawrence Oates was born in 1880 and fought in the Boer War. In 1910, he was elected to join Robert Scott's ill-fated expedition, and was one of five men who reached the

South Pole on 18th January, only to find they had been beaten there by a matter of weeks by a rival expedition led by the Norwegian, Amundsen.

All five perished on their return trip. Scott's diary records Oates' heroism. Suffering from frostbite and gangrene, he sacrificed himself so as not to slow down his companions. Uttering the now famous lines 'I am just going outside. I may be some time', he walked out of the tent into a blizzard.

The Oates Memorial Museum is at first floor level, while the collections relating to White are located on the ground floor. There are pieces of the great naturalist's furniture, as well as his letters and portraits of his family. It is in the garden, very much as he

UPPER WIELD

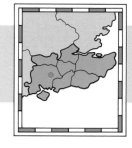

◄ *In largely unspoilt Upper Wield, thatched, flint-knapped cottages overlook a well kept village pond. The colourful spear thistle (inset) attracts butterflies with its sweet, musky odour.*

A thatched village and an old road in the Hampshire Downs

Set in the undulating landscape of the North Downs is the timeless village of Upper Wield, where thatched cottages cluster round a green and a pond. Hidden down a side lane is a delightful though heavily restored example of a small Norman church **Ⓐ**. It is dedicated to St James the Great.

13TH-CENTURY MURALS

The church was built by William the Conqueror's grandson, Henry de Blois, who was Bishop of Winchester. Scratched into the stonework beside the main door is a mass dial, a primitive sundial used before clocks were invented. Inside are 13th-century wall paintings depicting scenes from Christ's life, and a gallery that housed the band before the days of the organ.

The fine tomb by the altar commemorates William and Marjory Waloppe, who, in 1591, entertained Elizabeth I at Wield House. The house survives, much changed, and still retains its Tudor porch.

Not far from the village, across expansive fields, runs The Ox Drove **Ⓑ**. This ancient road between Winchester and Odiham was used for driving sheep to market. It may have been in use as early as the Roman occupation, and was part of King John's regular route between his castles at Winchester and Windsor. He built Odiham Castle at the exact halfway point of the 60-mile (96-km) route, two days' riding at that time. He is known to have passed along this way in 1215, the year he agreed to sign Magna Carta.

PRESTON HOUSE

As the drove approaches a disused chalk pit there is a view to the left, across the fields, to the early 17th-century Preston House. It is one of three mansions built to house the major landowners of the neighbouring parish of Preston Candover, after the enclosures there.

Lower Wield is not a great deal lower than Upper Wield. The name they share is a variation of 'weald', meaning open or wooded country, and they are in fact part of the same parish. Upper Wield had the church, and Lower Wield the pubs. The Windmill pub has become a cattery, but The Yew Tree **Ⓒ**, a 300-year-old pub sited by an old chalk pit, remains family-owned.

The path back into Upper Wield passes the back of the old village school **Ⓓ**, built to accommodate 50 children. Their longest holiday always coincided with the harvest. The school is now closed, but the building remains an important part of community life as the village hall.

FACT FILE

- ✳ Upper Wield, 5½ miles (8.8km) west of Alton

- ▭ Pathfinders 1244 (SU 63/73) & 1224 (SU 64/74), grid reference SU 628387

  miles 0 1 2 3 4 5 6 7 8 9 10 miles
  kms 0 1 2 3 4 5 6 7 8 9 10 11 12 13 14 15 kms

- 🕒 3 hours

- ▬ Mostly field paths over downland. Two gradual ascents

- 🅿 In turning off green opposite village noticeboard

- 🍴 Shop at Upper Wield and inn at Lower Wield

► *Incised into the stonework of Upper Wield's church is a mass dial, a primitive form of sundial.*

THE WALK

UPPER WIELD – LOWER WIELD

The walk begins at Upper Wield's church Ⓐ.

1 Go past the church door and bear half right to an exit in the corner of the churchyard. Turn right past the end of a barn and over a stile. At the next stile, continue ahead along a field edge to a kissing-gate. Go clockwise round the edge of the field; at the second corner cross a stile and continue ahead through a gate into a lane.

2 Turn left to Wield Wood Estate Sheep Dairy. Just beyond the main entrance, go left through a wooden gate and ahead to a narrow gate. Go through the small enclosure to a stile. Follow the path half right down the sloping field and cross a stile in a gap in the belt of trees. Continue half left across a field on a clear straight path. Where the path bears right, keep ahead on a narrow path cutting across the field

corner. The way passes through a gap in the trees to The Ox Drove Ⓑ.

3 Turn right and follow the bridleway for just over 1½ miles (2.4km).

4 As you approach a

wooded disused pit, turn right at an arrow on a tree to follow a less well defined path under an overhead cable and alongside a hedge. When the boundary ends keep ahead to a stile. Continue ahead to the corner of Park Copse. Follow the trees as the field narrows to a small gate. A narrow path swings through the trees to a stile. Continue ahead across a field to

another stile and walk through a plantation of young trees. Cross a track and a stile and follow the path ahead by a very high hedge and through a wood to stiles at a green lane.

5 Go ahead through the large garden of a thatched house to another stile behind a bush on the far side. Go half left, across a paddock divided by trees, to the far corner. Cross a stile into a garden with a

swimming pool. Walk half left past the right end of a white cottage and go through a rustic arch to the front drive which leads down to the road. Turn right along the Lower Wield lane passing, at a bend, Windmill Cattery.

6 At the second bend to the right, keep ahead through the bottom of a garden onto a path running down a field to a stile. A short path leads to a lane by the grass car park of The Yew Tree inn Ⓒ. Continue ahead up the side of a field. At the top, cross a stile and follow the unfenced path to come to a group of trees. An enclosed path runs ahead, passes the back of the school Ⓓ and returns to Upper Wield's green.

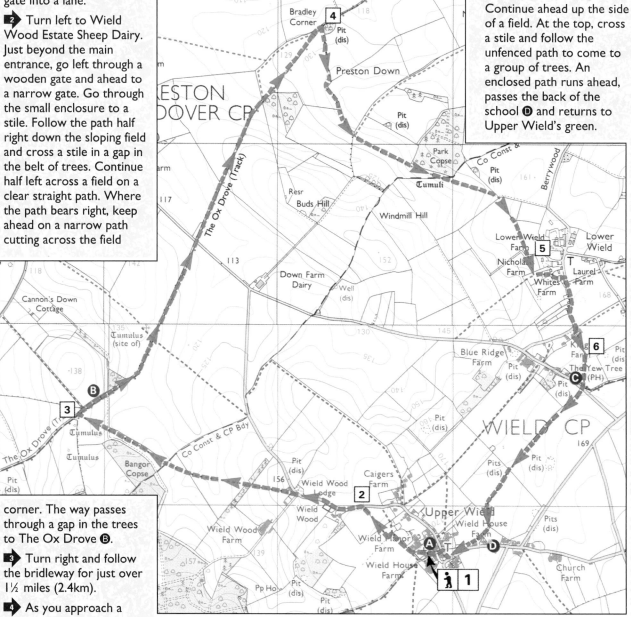

DEREK FORSS. INSET: COLIN CARVER/NATURE PHOTOGRAPHERS

FACT FILE

- ☀ Whitchurch, 6 miles (9.6km) east of Andover, just off the A34

- ▣ Pathfinder 1223 (SU 44/54), grid reference SU 461480

  miles 0 1 2 3 4 5 6 7 8 9 10 miles
  kms 0 1 2 3 4 5 6 7 8 9 10 11 12 13 14 15 kms

- ◕ Allow at least 3 hours

- ▬ Field paths and lanes. Some gentle slopes. Likely to be muddy after rain

- P Free parking off Bell Street

- T BR Whitchurch, Tel. (0171) 928 5100. Buses from Andover, Winchester and Basingstoke, Tel, (01256) 464501

- ⊞ Several pubs, cafés and restaurants in Whitchurch. The Watership Down Inn in Laverstoke. Tea-rooms at Silk Mill

- WC At the start

- ⌂ Whitchurch Silk Mill is open to the public, Tel. (01256) 893882

Explore the lovely Test Valley and its buildings

▲*As you follow the ancient Harroway out of Whitchurch, the route crosses chalky farmland. Rabbits (inset) can be seen here, in countryside where incidents in* **Watership Down** *were set.*

The charming countryside around Hampshire's sparkling River Test provides the setting for this walk. The river teems with trout. In the Middle Ages, its waters drove the wheels of corn-mills. Since the 18th century, they have powered silk, woollen and paper mills. Those still standing are among the finest industrial buildings in the county.

Whitchurch is tucked away in a fold of the chalk hills. There was a Saxon settlement here, with a church and possibly a minster, though all that remains from those times is a gravestone in the Parish Church of

All Hallows **Ⓐ**. This priceless relic, about 11 centuries old, was found embedded in the north wall in 1868. It is a memorial to a lady who may have been a nun at nearby Wherwell Priory. The stone has a carving of Jesus holding a book and raising his hand in blessing. Its Latin inscription translates as 'Here lies the body of Frithburga, buried in peace'.

The church, much restored in the 19th century, has a unique, 15th-century wooden staircase in the

▶*St Mary the Virgin is the parish church of Laverstoke and Freefolk.*

tower. There is also an unusual 17th-century oil painting, illustrating the Ten Commandments along with the penalties for breaking them.

The painting was discovered in a wall during alterations to the White Hart Inn, in a room which had always been known as 'The Commandments Room', though

DEREK FORSS

THE WALK

WHITCHURCH – LAVERSTOKE

The walk starts in the public car park off Bell Street, close to the Old Brewery Inn.

1 Return to the town centre. Turn right to the Church of All Hallows **A**. Return to the town centre, and take the left turn after Bell Street, Newbury

Street. Pass Denning House **B** on your left and go up the hill to the junction with Dances Lane.

2 Bear right up Dances Lane, which becomes a rough lane, with a row of houses on the left. Where it turns sharply left into a tarmac road, climb the stile by the metal gate in front of you, and cross the field to a stile in the far left corner. Go over it and under the railway bridge.

3 Climb a stile immediately right, and follow the footpath along the right field edge. Cross a stile and turn right onto a lane (Harroway). Just after a lane comes in from the right, take a cart-track

slightly right, which very soon joins another lane. Turn right.

4 Cross the railway line by South View Cottages, and take the next lane left. After 200 yards (180m), turn right on a signposted footpath across the field, towards the swings. The path goes through the playground of a disused school, and emerges by the Church of St Mary the Virgin **C**. Continue down the lane to the B3400.

5 Turn right to view the thatched cottages **D** (continue in this direction to visit the Watership Down Inn). Return along the B3400. Cross the Test and go past the entrance to

Laverstoke House **E** to Laverstoke Mill **F**.

6 Retrace your steps along the main road. Just before the Old Rectory, turn left on a signposted footpath along the edge of the garden. Cross a stile, with the Church of St Nicholas, Freefolk **G** on your right. The route continues left up the lane towards a house.

7 The lane curves to the left past the house, and a wooden kissing-gate is soon visible on your right. Follow a path across the fields, with the field boundary on your left. Continue walking through a belt of old oak trees. Climb a stile to cross a

field, towards a house.

8 The footpath passes to the left of the house, over stiles and into a lane. Continue past Bere Mill **H**. After following a fence and a wall, climb the stile at the end and continue through a long pasture, with a belt of woodland on your left.

9 At the end of the pasture, climb the stile in the top right corner (not left). Take a path with an overgrown slope along its left side. Continue beside open fields. Cross a footbridge to see Town Mill **J** then recross to follow the same path.

10 The path emerges on McFaulds Way. Continue straight ahead. Opposite Alliston Way, turn right on a footpath between hedges. Go through a kissing-gate, and continue ahead to Winchester Street. Cross to visit Whitchurch Silk Mill **K**. On leaving the mill, turn left to return to the start in the town centre.

DEREK FORSS

prehistoric trackway. You may well see a charm of noisy goldfinches here in summer, feeding on the seed-heads of the plentiful thistles.

You will also probably spot a few rabbits; this rolling countryside was the setting for Richard Adams' epic, *Watership Down*. The route crosses the railway (the rabbits' 'iron road') and eventually the Test (the 'great river' negotiated by the rabbits at Laverstoke).

At Freefolk, the route passes the Victorian Church of St Mary the

▼*In Freefolk you pass these almshouses with their lovely gardens and then come to the tiny, de-commissioned Church of St Nicholas (left).*

DEREK FORSS

nobody knew why. The painting may well have been hidden there during the Civil War.

The White Hart is an old coaching inn, and stood on the routes from Salisbury to London and from Oxford to Winchester. The position of Whitchurch, at a river crossing where two major routes met, made it one of the largest towns in Hampshire by the 16th century.

FAMOUS SON

One of the town's most illustrious residents is Lord Denning, former Master of the Rolls. A plaque marks his birthplace **B**, 5 Newbury Street, where his parents had a drapers' shop. He was taught at the current Old School House in London Street.

After leaving Whitchurch, the route picks up the Harroway, a

Nature Walk

WATER MILLS are sited on chalk streams, because their even flow keeps the wheel turning at a regular rate.

RICHARD PHIPPS

FLOATING BOARDS are strung in the stream by angling associations in order to encourage insect life, which in turn encourages trout.

Virgin **C**, and the old school, now closed, which dates back to 1850. A short detour takes you to a curious row of 18 half-thatched cottages **D**. These almshouses were built by Lord Portal in 1939 in an Arts and Crafts style, although they could be mistaken for much older houses.

The route passes the entrance to Laverstoke Park and the driveway

DEREK FORSS

▲*This elegant bridge crosses the shallow Test near Bere Mill (right), which Henri Portal once leased. The mill is no longer in commercial use and is not open to the public.*

SUE MORRIS

to Laverstoke House **E**, built in the 18th century in the Classical Revival style by Joseph Bonomi. The park is known for its suberb beech trees. Both house and grounds are private.

The clear, iron-free water of chalk streams, such as the Test, was ideal for paper-making. Laverstoke Mill **F** was acquired by Henri de Portal,

◄ *Town Mill in Whitchurch, once a flour-mill, is another of the Test's mills that has been converted into a private house.*

a French Huguenot refugee, who built a new mill there in 1718. In 1724, he gained a contract to supply the Bank of England with paper for bank-notes; in 1950, production was moved from Laverstoke to another Portal mill at nearby Overton. The present Laverstoke Mill is used for the development of water-filtering processes, amid high security.

The tiny 13th-century Church of St Nicholas, Freefolk **G** was the parish church until 1896. It is now maintained by the Redundant Churches Fund. It contains an impressive monument to Sir Richard Powlett, depicted reclining in armour with his two daughters.

Further along is Bere Mill **H**, a picturesque weatherboarded house. This was the first Portal's paper

mill, where Henri perfected his paper-making skills. It is a lovely spot from which to watch the trout swimming in the clear-running Test, by the 18th-century brick bridge.

The return route affords glimpses of the glittering Test and watercress beds through trees to your right. Town Mill **J**, standing over the river, was a flour-mill. The attractive weatherboarded building and water-wheel can be viewed from a footbridge over the swirling waters.

SILK ROUTE

Whitchurch Silk Mill **K**, near the end of the walk, is on an island in the Test. It was built around 1800 on the site of an ancient corn mill. In 1816, the mill was sold and then used for the hand weaving of wool, but it turned to silk production in about 1830. It has been restored to working order by the Hampshire Buildings Preservation Trust .

Whitchurch Silk

Making silk fabrics has always been an extremely labour-intensive process.

Whitchurch Silk Mill is the last working silk mill in England to still use old machinery. The earliest references to silk production at Whitchurch date from 1830. By 1838, the mill employed 108 people, including 39 children under the age of 13. In 1986, Hampshire Buildings Preservation Trust bought the mill from Ede and Ravenscroft, gown-makers to the legal profession.

The original power for the mill came from the River Test. The present wheel, made up of elm floats on a cast-iron frame, was installed in 1890. It turned a leather belt that drove 16 looms, and warping and winding machines, as well as an electrical generator for the lighting. At present, only the warping and winding machines are water-powered.

Raw silk, wound from the cocoons

of Chinese silk-worms, is reeled into hanks and sent to dyers in Suffolk and Essex. At Whitchurch, the hanks of coloured silk are wound onto wooden bobbins, which are then placed on a 'creel' holder; the silk from each bobbin is transferred onto a warp roll by the warping mill.

The individual strands of silk are wound on to the warp roll to its full width, and the full roll carried downstairs to the looms ready for weaving. The warp roll can take two or three days to enter on the loom, as each thread has to be individually wound onto its counterpart on the old warp, and there can be as many as 200 threads to the inch (2.5cm). Once the warp is set up, the shuttle carries the weft thread back and forth to create the finished fabric.

Making silk this way is very labour-intensive, and Whitchurch's success is built on providing small clients with specialist fabrics in short runs. As well as heavy black Ottoman for barristers' gowns, the mill produces a wide range of customized silks for use in films, opera and the theatre, as well as unique taffeta designs for curtains for interior designers and National Trust properties.

HAMPSHIRE

CAROLINE BACON. INSET: DEREK WASHINGTON/NATURE PHOTOGRAPHERS

Walking to a revealing hill fort and alongside a famous trout stream

There has been a bridge across the River Test at the west end of Stockbridge since the 15th century. The town's broad main street, built in 1200 on a chalk causeway across the valley, was wide enough to accommodate the 'stock' of the town's name — sheep and cattle driven down each year from the Welsh hills to the markets and fairs of south-eastern England.

Stockbridge is best known today for trout fishing, although the rights are owned by syndicates, and are not open to the public. The famous Houghton Fishing Club, founded in 1822, meets in the Grosvenor Hotel, whose porch extends into the street.

This building had another function in the 19th century: when the Stockbridge races were held on land between Danebury Hill and the river, the hotel belonged to Tom Cannon, who trained and raced his own horses, and it was here

▲*This disused water mill is on the River Anton and is passed on the walk at Fullerton. Marsh helleborine (inset), which flowers in summer, is an orchid that grows in waterside meadows.*

FACT FILE

✳ Stockbridge, 6 miles (9.6km) south of Andover, on the A3057

▭ Pathfinder 1242 (SU 23/33), grid reference SU 358350

miles 0 1 2 3 4 5 6 7 8 9 10 miles
kms 0 1 2 3 4 5 6 7 8 9 10 11 12 13 14 15 kms

◗ Allow at least 5 hours

▭ Easy walking on well defined paths and tracks

🅿 Along the main street in Stockbridge

🍴 Several pubs in Stockbridge; the Mayfly at Testcombe

wc In Stockbridge and in the car park at Danebury Hill

I Tourist Information Centres at Andover and Romsey

that the jockeys used to meet.

The route follows the main road west through the town. On the wall of the former inn called the Drovers' House Ⓐ is a charming reminder of the drove trade. An inscription in Welsh advertises 'seasoned hay, tasty pastures, good beer and comfortable beds'.

You climb Meon Hill along an enclosed track and cross Houghton Down. In the early 19th century, there was a racecourse here. A mile (1.6km) to the west are Chattis Hill Stables, a former racing establishment now used by a riding school.

REVEALING EXCAVATIONS

From the track below Blackstake Hill, there is a fine view of Danebury Hill, which you approach via a road. The hill fort Ⓑ crowing the summit has been systematically excavated over many years by a team of archaeologists, and gives one of the clearest pictures yet of life in an Iron Age settlement.

Danebury was built in about 550BC and housed several hundred people. Over the centuries, the outer walls were made more complex,

THE WALK

STOCKBRIDGE – DANEBURY HILL – LECKFORD

The walk starts by the roundabout at the east end of the main street.

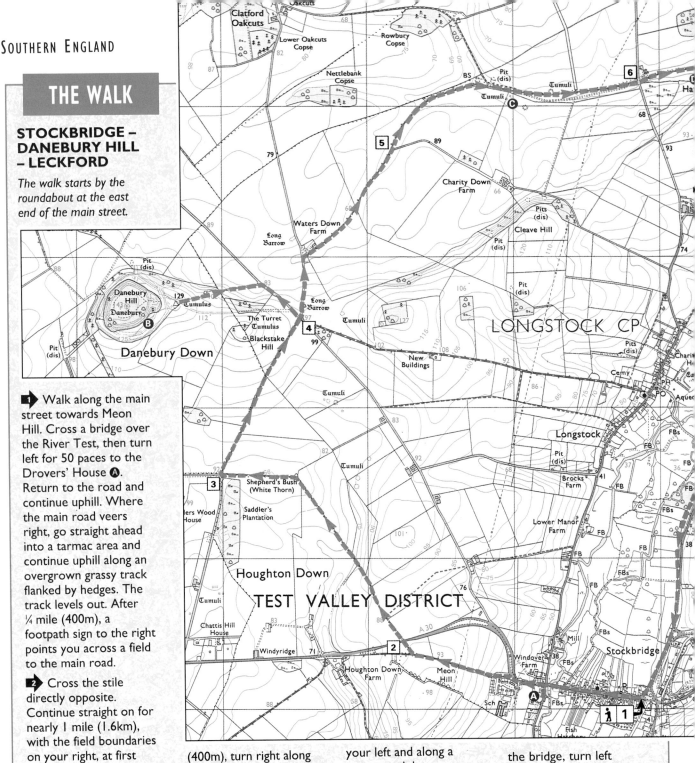

1 ▶ Walk along the main street towards Meon Hill. Cross a bridge over the River Test, then turn left for 50 paces to the Drovers' House **A**. Return to the road and continue uphill. Where the main road veers right, go straight ahead into a tarmac area and continue uphill along an overgrown grassy track flanked by hedges. The track levels. After ¼ mile (400m), a footpath sign to the right points you across a field to the main road.

2 ▶ Cross the stile directly opposite. Continue straight on for nearly 1 mile (1.6km), with the field boundaries on your right, at first slightly downhill then up a slope, on a broad track. At the top, follow the field boundary left, to a stile into a lane.

3 ▶ Turn right and continue to a main road.

4 ▶ Turn left. After ¼ mile (400 metres), turn left into the lane to Danebury Hill Fort **B**. Return to stage 4 and go left down a road signposted 'Red Rice and Andover'. After ¼ mile

(400m), turn right along a broad track, passing a farm building on your left. Continue along the track until it turns right at a metal gate saying 'Private Road'.

5 ▶ Veer left on the grassy path. Just after a path joins from the left, note the tumuli **C** on your right. Continue walking to a road.

6 ▶ Cross, and follow the footpath sign ahead, past a metal barn on

your left and along a grassy track between low hedges. Continue, with the slopes of Hazel Down **D** on your right, to another road.

7 ▶ Turn left. Go through Fullerton and turn right at a T-junction. Walk past the old mill **E** on your right, and over a bridge. At the main road, turn right. Beyond the Mayfly, cross another bridge.

8 ▶ Immediately after

the bridge, turn left along a road signposted 'Chilbolton'. After 50 paces, turn right along the footpath marked Test Way. To see the village of Leckford **F**, go onto the road and turn left where the path and the road run close together just past the houses.

9 ▶ Return to the path and continue until it emerges onto the main road. Follow the verge back into Stockbridge.

BOTH PHOTOS: CAROLINE BACON

until huge, twisting ramparts round the main gate made hostile entry a dangerous enterprise. The principal weapons used by the defenders were slingshots; huge ammunition piles of small round stones were discovered near the entrance.

Circular wooden huts were grouped behind the ramparts, and in the centre were several religious buildings. The rest of the site was used to store grain, either in pits cut into the chalk or in raised granaries.

In 100BC the fort was abandoned. The main east gate was burnt at this time, which suggests that it succumbed to an attack. The site remained deserted until the Middle Ages, when it became the venue for

▼*Now a quiet private dwelling, the Drovers' House was once a noisier, lively inn for Welsh cattle drovers.*

an annual fair.

Later, it was used as a rabbit warren; the remains of trenches and the warrener's hut were discovered by the archaeologists. At the turn of the 20th century, it was a useful place from which to watch the races. Although the racecourses have gone now, the views of Hampshire from the summit are still magnificent.

There are relics of an earlier community along the next stretch, which follows a broad track through the undulating downland scenery. At several places along the path are ancient barrows and burial mounds **C**, dating from the Neolithic to the Bronze Age (4000-700BC). They are often covered in trees or bushes; farmers generally find it easier to plough round them.

DOWNLAND FLORA

The broad ridges on the side of Hazel Down **D** are known as lynchets, and date from the Middle Ages. They were formed when slopes were ploughed; the loose soil slid downhill to make a bank. Sometimes these terraces were large enough to support woodland.

Many plant species grow on the chalk downland, including bastard toadflax, horseshoe vetch and the attractive bee orchid. These, in turn, are a breeding ground for a multitude of butterflies. On a fine day in

▲*These mounds are the surviving earthworks around the main gate at the Iron Age fort on top of Danebury Hill.*

summer, the air is full of chalkhill blues and meadow browns.

The route continues gently down to flat meadowland by the River Test. Here, the scenery is very different from the open chalk hills. There are trees and woods, rich grass and a greenness not found on the higher ground.

You pass several picturesque cottages, including an old mill **E** where a bridge crosses the Anton, a tributary of the Test. You follow the main road for a short distance, passing the Mayfly pub, a welcome stopping place on a hot day.

Just beyond Testcombe Bridge, the route joins the Test Way, a long-distance path that runs the 50 miles (80km) from Totton in Southampton to Inkpen Beacon. In 1794, a canal was opened beside the river here. It joined Andover with Southampton, but was not a success and was soon abandoned. A railway was begun in 1857, and a junction at Fullerton was opened in 1885.

Part of the route, which was known as the 'Sprat and Winkle Line', ran along filled-in sections of the canal. The line had a brief rise to fame when, in 1927, it featured in a film of the play, *The Ghost Train*. It closed in the early 1960s, and the Test Way now follows its course from Fullerton to Stockbridge.

You continue towards Leckford **F**, a village owned entirely by the John Lewis Partnership. Here there are pheasant-rearing pens and fish nurseries, which help restock the river. In the 13th-century church are the remains of a cloister, reputedly part of a hospital owned by a

▶ *Looking from Testcombe Bridge there is a good chance of seeing trout in the crystal clear waters of the Test. At nearby Leckford there are some attractive thatched cottages (below).*

nunnery that existed in the area.

On the west side of the Test, and well worth a visit, is Longstock, an attractive village of thatched cottages. The water garden is open to the public once a month.

Behind Charity Farm, on private land, archaeologists have revealed a very interesting chapter in the history of the Test. A channel 300 feet (90m) long has been excavated alongside the river. It is thought to be a dock used by invading Danish longships as they made their way upstream from Southampton.

WANDERING RIVER

As the walk continues along the old railway line, the river is elusive; it glides from one side of the valley to the other, and is obscured by trees and tall reeds in summer. On the wetlands, meadowsweet, dropwort and marsh helleborine grow, and herons compete with the anglers for fish. The odd thatched fisherman's hut can be seen through the trees, with a view of downland beyond.

Finally, the route joins the main road and continues along the grassy verge back to Stockbridge.

ALL PHOTOS: CAROLINE BACON

Fishing on the Test

The River Test rises just east of the village of Overton and flows south, through Stockbridge and Romsey, to reach the sea at Southampton Water. The chalk stream is famous throughout the world for its trout, but it also supports other fish, notably salmon and eels. In 1882, a salmon weighing 43lb (19.5kg), some 3 feet (90cm) in circumference and 4 feet (1.2m) long, was caught downstream from Romsey.

From late August onwards, eels are netted as they swim back to the sea. The nets stretch right across the width of the river, and can be seen from the road that crosses the Test near Longstock.

Nearby is a fine example of the picturesque fishermen's thatched huts that grace the river north of Stockbridge. These huts were built by the Houghton Fishing Club, one of the most exclusive clubs in the country. Founded in 1822, it has a record of every fish caught, cataloguing who caught it, and what type of fly they used.

The club's members meet in the Grosvenor Hotel in Stockbridge, and their main interest is trout. In the early days of the club, coarse fish such as pike were caught; these have now been all but eliminated.

In 1877, F M Halford made a detailed study of fish and their food, and, as a result, created dry

(artificial) flies in meticulous detail. These were a huge success. Since then, dry fly fishing has been a major feature of the Houghton Club.

Another individual to make a significant contribution to the management of the river was William Lunn, who came to Stockbridge at the instigation of the Secretary of the Houghton Club in 1886, and remained river keeper there for 45 years. He was the inventor of the fly board, a floating plank on which mayfly can breed, with their larvae being kept safe from land-living predators. The board is still used in fisheries.

Today, there are a number of nurseries where fish are reared to restock the river. However, despite careful management and improved technology, few catches can match those made in the last century, and it would appear that fishing is in decline on the River Test.

A thatched fisherman's hut in the middle of a row of basketwork eel traps on the Test.

From Carisbrooke village to the hilltop castle

The ancient village of Carisbrooke winds uphill above the valley of the Lukely Brook. Its oldest building is a Roman villa which is currently being restored in the grounds of the vicarage. And the narrow High Street is dominated by the towering ramparts of the castle **C** to the south and the Norman church of St Mary **A** on its hillock to the north.

Once a Benedictine Priory stood to the north of the church but it was suppressed as 'foreign' in 1415. Some of its stones were used in the

▶ *The castle, built on the site of a Roman fort, dominates Carisbrooke.*

ENGLISH HERITAGE

FACT FILE

* Carisbrooke, south-west of Newport, Isle of Wight

* Outdoor Leisure Map 29, grid reference SZ 486882

| miles 0 | 1 | 2 | 3 | 4 | 5 | 6 | 7 | 8 | 9 | 10 miles |
| kms 0 | 1 2 | 3 | 4 5 | 6 | 7 8 | 9 | 10 11 | 12 | 13 14 | 15 kms |

* Allow 1 ¹/₂ hours

* Mostly easy. One stony farm track, so good walking shoes are recommended

* **P** On the south side of the B3401 in the centre of Carisbrooke village

* **T** Buses from Newport stop beside the car park

* The village offers a range of cafés, restaurants, a wine bar and tea room

* **WC** At car park

* Carisbrooke Castle, overlooking Carisbrooke village. There is an admission charge. The castle is open all year except at Christmas and New Year

building of Priory Farm and the great tower of St Mary's Church.

FLOWERS AND BIRDS

Carisbrooke was once famous for its mills. The old pond of Priory Mill **B** has been turned by the former Southern Water Board into a beautiful, willow-fringed lake, with benches and picnic tables along its banks. It is a cool haven on a hot day — for mallard, swans and even the occasional kingfisher.

After visiting the lake, the walk passes a stream and enters Spring Lane. This path leads up to a beech wood where jays and magpies scold high up in the branches. Beyond lie the wide turf moats of the castle's outer defences where the blue

▼ *The entrance and gatehouse to the castle. (inset) Viper's bugloss was once thought to be a cure for snake bites.*

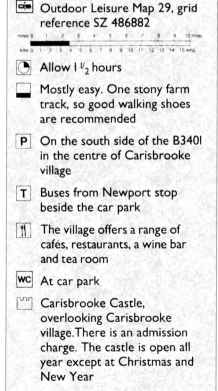

ENGLISH HERITAGE. INSET: PAUL STERRY/NATURE PHOTOGRAPHERS

THE WALK

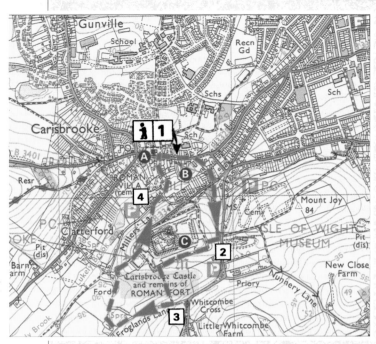

CARISBROOKE

The walk begins at the central car park on the south side of Carisbrooke High Street or the bus stop from Newport close by.

1 Cross Carisbrooke High Street to the north side by the pelican crossing, turning up the steps to the churchyard **A**. After visiting the church, turn right out of porch and take any narrow path between the graves leading to back of church and circle back to steps, regaining High Street. Walk down this road until opposite a ford. Cross the road with care and at once turn through a gateway on the right, leading over a footbridge to a lake, Priory Mill **B**. After visiting the lake return to the gateway and turn right along a stream into Spring Lane. Follow this to a T-junction and carefully cross the road and continue straight on, now following a sunken path under beech trees. (For a short cut to Castle, turn right up steps and keep straight on.)

2 At the top, turn right along a short lane emerging on to grassy moats round Castle, keeping left along them almost to a right-angled turn. Go left down a steep bank into a straight, narrow path. Cross the stile and at the end of the path turn right at a farm lane.

3 Continue along lane and take first turning on right. This leads to a water-splash with footbridge, then to a junction of four lanes. Take first lane on right, a steep chalk track signposted Carisbrooke Castle — this emerges in the castle car park. Continue ahead in the same direction to reach castle entrance **C** on the right. Otherwise, continue just beyond the traffic lights and turn left down steps signed to church and shops. Then follow diagonal path across meadow to stile in corner leading on to a very short path and out into Millers Lane.

4 Turn right along the lane and keep straight on, ignoring turning to right, and walk along beside a stream, emerging into narrow Castle Street which makes a T-junction with Carisbrooke High Street opposite the church. Turn right and continue along pavement to find the car park in a few yards, or the bus stop for Newport opposite.

spikes of viper's bugloss grow on the walls, with cowslips beneath them. Inside grow such rarities as green alkanet and the white orchid, autumn lady's tresses. Kestrels hover over ancient bastions and towards evening, little owls screech out from the battlements. And from the moat there is a wide view of central Wight. The lane walks ahead provide a taste of this green, unspoilt countryside

THE MEDIEVAL CASTLE

A steep chalk track leads towards Carisbrooke Castle. Though parts of the castle date back to Saxon times, it is most famous as the enforced home of King Charles I during the Civil War. There are also seven acres of buildings and ruins to explore and the island's museum.

The north side of the car park provides an impressive panoramic view of Carisbrooke. The Lukely Brook below runs through its lush water meadows – a silver thread that once drove three mills and maintained a thriving watercress industry. Above rise the red tiled roofs of the village, surmounted by the church, with fields spreading away beyond to Parkhurst Forest, where kings once hunted.

The walk ends in Castle Street – a picturesque lane of old cottages with the Lukely Brook running along part of its length and fine views of the church and Carisbrooke Castle.

◄ *St Mary's Church in Carisbrooke. (inset) In the castle there is a donkey-operated wheel for drawing well water.*

J. ALLAN CASH. INSET: WOODMANSTERNE

◀ *The chalk downs of Freshwater Bay command breathtaking views of the English Channel. Much of the area is now owned by the National Trust and wildlife, including the common spotted orchid (inset), flourishes.*

FACT FILE

✳	Freshwater Bay, Isle of Wight (West Wight)
🖳	Outdoor Leisure Map 29, grid reference SZ 345858

miles 0 1 2 3 4 5 6 7 8 9 10 miles
kms 0 1 2 3 4 5 6 7 8 9 10 11 12 13 14 15 kms

◐	Allow a full day for your visit, including 2 hours for walk
▭	Very easy with one short, rather steep climb at the beginning of the walk
P	In country car park, Freshwater Bay
T	The Isle of Wight can be reached by ferry from Lymington, there is a frequent ferry service: Lymington – Yarmouth. Regular bus service to Freshwater Bay from Yarmouth and Newport
WC	Beside bus stop at the start of the walk
🍴	All facilities in Freshwater Bay including pub, tea rooms and beach trays

A downland walk within sight and sound of the sea

Although there is only a small village at Freshwater Bay **Ⓐ**, it has become famous because of its beautiful setting. The little bay is framed by a semi-circle of sheer white cliffs, which rise to sweeping downlands. To the right of the Bay are three prominent rocks named the Arch, Stag and Mermaid.

POET LAUREATE

This magical little Bay has appealed to many eminent people apart from its most famous resident, Alfred Tennyson. George Bernard Shaw began writing *Caesar and Cleopatra* here, Virginia Woolf wrote a play *Freshwater* about Tennyson and his friends, Charles Darwin stayed in the village and the pioneer photographer, Julia Margaret Cameron made her home at the cottage named 'Dimbola' in the main street.

The lovely seaward down next to Freshwater Bay, Tennyson Down **Ⓑ**, has been named after Tennyson, the Poet Laureate of the Victorian Age,

HEATHER ANGEL

LAURIE CAMPBELL/NHPA

▲ *The ring ouzel is one of the downland species seen in West Wight. A shy bird, it often perches on far-off rocks.*

THE WALK

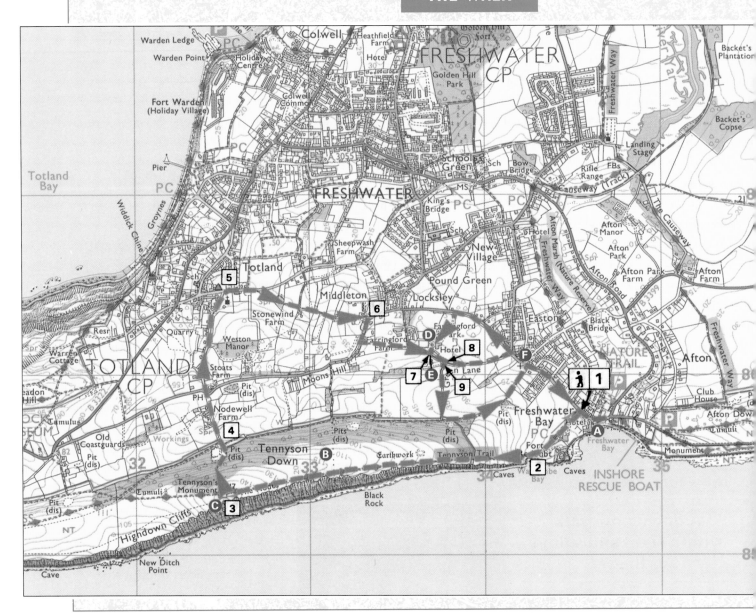

Celtic Memorial Cross

The route of this walk along the cliff tops west of Freshwater Bay was the daily walk of Alfred, Lord Tennyson from his house at Farringford. The Celtic cross was erected in 1897 as a memorial to the poet and it bears the inscription 'In memory of Alfred Lord Tennyson. This was raised as a Beacon to Sailors by the people of Freshwater and other Friends in England and America.'

Most of the downland is now owned by the National Trust and contains a wealth of wildlife.

because he walked here almost daily during the forty years from 1853 when he lived at Farringford close by. He said the air was 'worth sixpence a pint'. Among the most famous poems he composed here are *The Charge of the Light Brigade* and *The Idylls of the King*.

INDIGENOUS WILDLIFE

As you follow the gentle rise of the down the whole western approaches are spread before you. There are wonderful views, left over the Channel and right over the Solent. Preserved by the National Trust, the down is rich in grasses and flowers, which include vetches, cowslips, harebells, pyramid and bee orchids,

FRESHWATER BAY

A circular walk beginning from Freshwater Bay **Ⓐ** *in West Wight. The walk can start from the car park close to the beach or from the bus stop a short distance away close to the large hotel in the bay.*

1 From the car park walk beside the road with the beach on your left and follow the sign for the Needles Pleasure Park and Old Battery. Walk up the road with the Albion Hotel on your left and turn left just before the bus shelter following the sign for Fort Redoubt. From the bus stop walk a few yards down the road towards the beach and turn right at the Fort Redoubt sign.

2 Follow the lane until it turns left for Fort Redoubt tea rooms. Leave the lane here and walk straight ahead passing through a squeeze-barrier at right of gate. Bear right along the top of the cliff (Watcombe Bay) and go through a barrier beside the next gate. Follow the path ahead as it climbs to the top of the Tennyson Down **Ⓑ**. The correct direction is now straight ahead but you can either follow the fence or follow a path closer to the cliff edge. (Take care not to go too close to the edge as the chalk is unstable). Keep to this magnificent downland way (views south over the Channel and north over the Solent) for over a mile (1.6 km) until you come to the tall granite Celtic cross erected in memory of Alfred Tennyson **Ⓒ**.

3 There is no clear path for about 100 yards (90 metres) from the Memorial Cross. With your back to the Cross and the Channel walk straight ahead down the grassy slope towards a fringe of low trees and shrubs. Now you will see a clear path running downhill through the trees. The chalky surface can be very slippery. Follow the path as it runs steeply down through attractive woods into a valley. Keep to the path as it bears to the right of a disused chalk quarry, between bushes to a footpath sign.

4 Do not follow the footpath running left but bear slightly right down a metalled lane passing the cottages at Nodewell. With Highdown Inn on your left, cross straight over the minor road (Alum Bay Old Road) and follow the lane opposite for about 700 yards (650 metres) to another minor road.

5 Turn right past the church and walk a short distance up the road to a kissing-gate and footpath sign on your right. Turn right through the gate and follow the direction of the sign, half-left, to a small copse. Cross the stile, walk through the trees and leave the copse by another stile. Follow the path with a fence on your right to a gate and stile. Cross the stile and keep straight on up the lane ahead. Keep to the lane as it runs between high banks of ferns to the minor road at Moons Hill.

6 Cross the road and turn right uphill for about 100 yards (90 metres). Look carefully along the hedge on left for a kissing-gate and footpath sign by an electricity pole. Turn left through the gate following the sign for Tennyson Down and Gate Lane. Bear right and walk up the field keeping the hedge close on your right. Ahead you can see Farringford Home farm and Farringford House **Ⓓ**. Cross the stile at the far end of the field and follow the lane, through the gate, straight ahead with the grounds of Farringford on your left.

7 Walk under Tennyson's small wooden bridge **Ⓔ** and another bridleway joins our path on the right. This is Tennyson's path to the High Down and your way back to Freshwater Bay but first you might like to visit Farringford, Tennyson's home for much of his life.

8 Do not turn right towards the High Down but keep straight on to the road running down to Freshwater Bay. Turn left and follow Bedbury Lane. Turn left up the drive to Farringford (now hotel). For the price of a drink you will be made welcome and shown Tennyson's study containing personal memorabilia. Retrace your steps to the bridleway leading to the High Down.

9 Turn right (left if you visited Farringford) and follow the bridleway towards the Down. A steep white path leads ahead up the Down, but you bear left keeping to your terraced path as it runs along the foot of the Down through the valley. Follow the path to a gate. Pass through the side of the gate and keep to the path along the field edge straight ahead towards Freshwater Bay. Over the field to the left you will see the lovely little thatched church of St Agnes **Ⓕ**. Our path meets the road beside the church. Turn right to walk back to the car park by the beach. Turn left to a request bus stop for a return journey to Yarmouth or Newport.

◀ *The view of Freshwater from Tennyson Down shows the thatched church of St Agnes in the foreground.*

quaking grass, yellow wort, carline thistles and autumn lady's tresses. Buzzards and kestrels quarter the down for rabbits, and smaller birds include meadow pipits, wheatears and ring ouzels. Uncommon seabirds nesting in the cliffs include guillemots, razorbills and puffins.

The first settlers farmed here about 3,800 BC. They have left the

◀ *This wooden bridge was built in Tennyson's garden at Farringford as his private escape route onto the Downs.*

Cameron and a case containing some of his personal belongings such as his black cloak and microscope. The poet could leave his study unobserved by way of an arched door and narrow staircase leading down to the garden.

Walking along the down back towards Freshwater the pretty church of St Agnes **F** is visible. It has something of the look of a country cottage, with its thatched roof broken by tiny dormer windows. The site for the church was given by Lord Tennyson, son of the Poet Laureate, and Lady Tennyson suggested the new church should be dedicated to St Agnes. The church was consecrated on 12th August, 1908. The church was constructed of stone from a local derelict farmhouse dating from 1694. An inscribed stone can be found incorporated in the vestry wall.

remains of an unfinished burial chamber, or long barrow, on the down. Later, Bronze Age tribes have raised their round burial mounds on the high down also. Continuing along the down one comes to Tennyson's Monument **C** . This tall granite Celtic cross was erected in 1897. After walking through woods and fields one comes across Farringford **D**, a late Georgian house with Gothic-style windows and castellated walls that was Alfred Tennyson's home from 1853 to his death in 1892. A friend described the house as being 'full of the sounds of birds and the distant sea'. From the windows Tennyson had a splendid view of Freshwater Bay and Compton Cliffs.

THE HIGH DOWN

If one visits Farringford (now a hotel) one can see the small wooden bridge **E** that Tennyson had built so that he could leave his garden, walk through a copse, and so reach the bridleway to the High Down unnoticed. He wrote how he loved to stand here in the evening:

'All by myself in my own dark
garden ground
Listening now to the tide in
its broad-flung shipwrecking roar.....'

Also, for those interested in the poet, Tennyson's study can be seen at Farringford (enquiries to the Farringford Tennyson society). Tennyson's study was the small room at the back of the house that he had enlarged into the airy, bow-windowed room we see today to house his many books. His desk, with the drawers stuffed with tobacco stood in the window. There are some fine portraits of the poet including one by Julia Margaret

Alfred Lord Tennyson

Tennyson was born at Somersby Rectory in the Lincolnshire wolds in 1809. From his earliest boyhood he knew he wanted to be a poet. He delighted in roaming the gentle countryside around his home and developed a keen eye for even the tiniest details of nature. Educated by his father and then at Trinity College, Cambridge he won the chancellor's medal for English verse in 1829. His friends included Arthur Hallam.

When Hallam died in 1833, Tennyson began what some people consider his greatest series of poems *In Memoriam*. Next to the Bible, Queen Victoria told him, *In Memoriam* had been her main source of comfort after the death of her beloved Prince Albert.

Tennyson gained more critical attention with books of verse, which included *The Lotus Eaters* and the *Morte d'Arthur*. Fame and prosperity came with the publication of *Maud* in 1855. (The proceeds also helped him to purchase Farringford, previously rented.) His marriage to Emily Sellwood in 1850, brought, he wrote, 'the peace of God into my life.'

Among Tennyson's many poems, his *Idylls of the King* must rank highly but perhaps his son, Hallam, was right when he called one simple and very beautiful poem the crown of his life's work. This was *Crossing the Bar*, which Tennyson wrote two years before his death, on the back of a used envelope, while he was travelling from Lymington to Yarmouth on the ferry. Tennyson died in 1892 and was buried in Westminster Abbey. He will always be honoured as the poet of the Victorian Age capturing its ideals in melodious and stirring verse. But he will also continue to give pleasure to all who enjoy the outdoors and share his keen observation of Nature in all her moods.

Farringford, a late-Georgian house, was Tennyson's home from 1852.

A walk through woods and downlands with views of the sea

The Isle of Wight is often described as England in miniature. This walk proves how true that is! You will find an old world manor house with beautiful gardens, oak woods carpeted with bluebells, high downland with magnificent sea views and green fertile valleys that have been farmed since Neolithic times. Traces of these early inhabitants remain. Also featured are a Neolithic tomb and megalith, barrow tombs raised in the early Bronze Age and a wooded hill crowned with the earthworks of an Iron Age fort. The woods and downs in this beautiful and undisturbed corner of the island contain a rich variety of plant and bird life.

The walk begins from the lovely village of Mottistone. The name

▲*Mottistone Down offers breathtaking views of countryside, sea and cliffs. The slow worm (inset), found in habitats with good vegetation cover, is a type of lizard, not a snake.*

DEREK PRATT. INSET: M.B. WITHERS/FRANK LANE PICTURE AGENCY

FACT FILE

* Mottistone, south-west Isle of Wight

os Outdoor Leisure Map 29, grid reference SZ 405837

miles 0 1 2 3 4 5 6 7 8 9 10 miles
kms 0 1 2 3 4 5 6 7 8 9 10 11 12 13 14 15 kms

◗ Allow 4 hours

▬ Fairly easy but some climbing

P Large National Trust car park beside Mottistone Manor

T Lymington-Yarmouth ferry (hourly). Then bus or car to Mottistone. Ring Southern Vectis (01983) 522456 for bus times

⊞ Facilities in Brightstone, also in Yarmouth and at Lymington ferry terminal

⊞ Mottistone Manor gardens, open to the public: Wednesdays and Bank Holiday Mondays 2–5.30pm, 5 April–27 September

'Mottistone' is probably derived from the Saxon word for a meeting place — a moot — which would be held close to the easily recognised Longstone on the hillside above.

Mottistone Manor Ⓐ, at the heart of the village, is a lovely, mainly 16th-century house built of multi-coloured Island stone. It has a recorded history dating back to the Domesday Book of 1086. You have a/ splendid view of the house and gardens on the walk.

THE LONGSTONE

After your ascent from the village you reach the Longstone Ⓑ. This huge pillar, 13 feet (4 metres) high, with another stone beside it, is the island's only megalith, dating from the New Stone Age, 3,500-2,500 BC. Behind the stone you can trace the outline of a large Neolithic tomb.

Walking towards the down you pass an area of reforestation. The Forestry Commission are felling a great many trees, mainly Corsican pine. These are being replaced with

DEREK PRATT

◀*Known as the Longstone, the two stones are formed of iron sandstone and date from the Neolithic period.*

THE WALK

MOTTISTONE – HIGH DOWNS

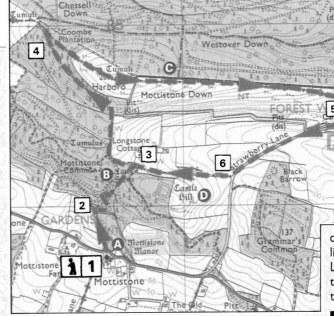

This circular walk starts from the car park beside Mottistone Manor **A** *or from the bus stop in front of the Manor. Approaching Mottistone from the west, you will see the car park signs (National Trust, Mottistone Manor) on the left just after the village sign. Approaching from the east, drive past the Manor and you will see the signs almost immediately on your right. Follow the gravel track to the parking area. From the car park walk, with the church on your right, down the steps to the footpath sign pointing left for the Longstone where you begin the walk. From the bus stop, walk west, with the Manor on your right, and turn right to pick up the footpath sign for the Longstone ahead of you.*

1 Follow the very pretty path as it winds gently uphill under the curving branches of trees.

2 When the path divides keep left. When path divides again at open area of felled trees, keep right along the winding path which ascends to a wide crossing track. Turn right along this track, with panoramic coastal views.

Look for steps on right and turn left immediately opposite them. Keep on steeply uphill until you come to a huge iron sandstone rock, with a smaller rock beside it, on your left. This is the Longstone **B**.

3 Just past the Longstone, turn left and follow the gravel track. When the track divides keep right. Ignore the next turning left and keep straight on towards the foot of the down. Keep to the main track as it bears left through cleared woodland. On left are glimpses of Brook Hill House, former home of the author J. B. Priestley.

4 Follow the track until you see a gate ahead.

About 50 yards (46 metres) before the gate you come to a wide crosstrack. Turn right, then almost immediately, turn right again. (At first, this path runs almost parallel with your path to the crosstrack.) Walk uphill towards a gate. Go through the gate and follow the wide, green way ahead along the top of Mottistone Down **C**.

5 The path descends to two gates. Go through both of them, pass a car park on your right, to a minor road. Bear right along the road for just a few paces, then sharp right down a narrow lane. Take great care as this narrow lane is a popular car route. Follow the lane as it drops steeply off the down to

cross the valley and climb a little at the other side. Look for a stile and gate on the right with footpath sign to the Longstone.

6 Turn right over the stile and follow the track. Mottistone Down is now on your right. Ahead of you, a little to your left, is Castle Hill **D**. Cross the next stile and continue along the track. You pass a thatched stone barn on your right and come to a stile with a red-brick farmhouse on your right. Cross the stile and walk over the track to the Longstone ahead. Retrace your earlier route from the Longstone to the crosstrack. Keep ahead over track and down steps. Follow path that meanders along the right of the valley, with good views of Mottistone Manor on left, finally bearing left down the original route to car park on your right. Turn left for your return to bus stop.

hardwoods, beech and sycamore.

The view from Mottistone Down **C** over a lovely valley to the sea is breathtaking. To the west are the white cliffs of Compton Bay and the whole of the eastern cliffs as far as St Catherine's Point lie to the east. Many Bronze Age burial mounds follow the crest of the down.

The last stretch of the route passes Castle Hill **D**. This hill is so called because Iron Age hill forts are

◄ *Green tunnels of luxuriant foliage lead from the hill path behind the 16th-century Mottistone Manor.*

often termed 'castles' though only the earth embankments remain.

This walk has a wide variety of habitats. The woods are full of bird-song; wrens, blackbirds, thrushes and woodpeckers are all likely to be seen. Primroses, bluebells and violets grow to form glowing carpets of colour. The National Trust is allowing the down to return to its natural state with low-growing flowers and shrubs. It is famous for its pipits, ring ouzels and falcons. The sides of the lanes are pitted with fox and rabbit holes and overhung with ladies' smock and wild arum.

A family walk through inland valleys with many historic attractions

This walk from the island's capital, Newport **Ⓐ**, leads over beautiful downland to discover some fascinating treasures, both natural and man-made. All members of the family should find something to interest them. You will see the remains of a Roman villa **Ⓑ** with a magnificently preserved bath suite, a country craft village **Ⓓ**, where the craftsmen can be watched at work in their studios and shops grouped around a village green, a Norman church with a centre where you can buy all you need to make your own brass rubbings, and one of the finest houses on the island, Arreton Manor **Ⓔ**, dating mainly from Elizabethan and Jacobean days. The house is the home of the

FACT FILE

✳ Newport, central Isle of Wight

os Outdoor Leisure 29, grid reference SZ 499889

miles 0 1 2 3 4 5 6 7 8 9 10 miles
kms 0 1 2 3 4 5 6 7 8 9 10 11 12 13 14 15 kms

◖ Allow a full day to include visits to attractions

▬ Easy, but includes one fairly steep climb

Ⓟ Long-stay car park: grid reference SZ 504892. Some quiet road parking south of bus station around Roman Villa area

🍴 Newport. Arreton Country Craft Village: licensed restaurant. Arreton Manor: teas, lunches, bar

⛫ Arreton Manor: open April to October

▲From St George's Down, woods and farmland are visible. The area around Arreton has fertile soil and grows much of the island's produce. Common centaury (inset), a member of the gentian family, flowers from June to October and grows in dry grass and dunes.

▼The fish pond at the back of Arreton Manor can be enjoyed after a visit to the many different museums that are housed in this beautiful, historic home.

THE WALK

NEWPORT – ARRETON

This circular walk begins from the bus station in Newport **A** *, the county town of the Isle of Wight. It is at the centre of a network of buses to all areas of the island. If parking in long-stay car park (grid reference SZ 504892), turn left along the main thoroughfare (South Street) to traffic lights and bus station.*

1 With your back to the bus station (looking towards the tower of St Thomas's Church), turn left to St James' Road. Turn left, follow St James' Road and continue up St John's Street until you come to Cypress Road on your left (ignore earlier sign to the Roman Villa). Turn left down Cypress Road to visit the Roman Villa **B**, the entrance to which is on the left-hand side of the road. Return to St John's Road and continue to mini-roundabout, then straight ahead up Watergate Road until you come to the entrance to Watergate School on your left, and a Public Footpath sign. Turn left and follow the path through a little gate to the left of the school entrance. The path leads round the school, past Shide Dairy and down to the road, the B3407.

2 Turn right and cross the bridge over the Medina river, passing The Barley Mow pub on your left. Cross the main road (A3020) towards the 'Blackwater Road' sign. Keep straight on for a few yards, then bear right up St George's Lane, which climbs steeply to the top of St George's Down. Keep on past the sign that tells you that you are following

the Bembridge Trail, the Old Highway to Arreton Cross.

3 At the top of the down, keep on along the track that bears a little right along the top of the ridge, leaving the road marked 'Quarry Vehicles only' and the entrance to the golf clubhouse on your left. About 80 yards (73 metres) past the clubhouse you will see a stile on your left. You cross this at the end of the walk to rejoin St George's Lane. Keep on along the crest of the down as it bears left, ignoring all footpath signs on the right. For the earlier part of the way you have the golf course on your left and a quarry on your right.

4 Cross straight over the track that leads to the quarry and keep on along the Bembridge Trail, which bears left and climbs to give a wonderful view **C** over the Arreton Valley and the south of the Island. Keep on following the Old Highway and Arreton signs. The path now starts to descend a little and sinks deep between high banks laced with tree roots.

5 At this point there is a post with five footpath signs, which can be confusing. You have a choice of paths here, both running in the same direction to almost the same point. If you wish, you can carry straight on down the sunken path. The alternative route to Arreton village is a path running along the edge of the fields to the left. If you wish to follow this, bear slightly left of the main track and cross the stile on your right into the field. This is signposted with a yellow arrow, public footpath to Arreton. Continue down the field edges crossing two more stiles. Both ways bring you down to the main road.

Cross, and follow the A3056 signposted to Sandown, Shanklin and Ventnor (there is a wide grass verge) the short distance to Arreton village. On the left you will see the sign to Arreton Craft Village **D**.

6 Ignore the first sign for Arreton Manor and continue past the White Lion pub. Now turn left as indicated for the 12th-century church and brass rubbing centre. This route takes you past lovely stone-built houses, the church, which is on your right (signposted 'A12 footpath to Manor and the Downs') and then to the right of some farm buildings. The path now bears left to a footpath sign (Arreton

Manor and Robin Hill) then turns right to begin to climb to Arreton Down.

7 Before the path turns right, look carefully for a small iron gate on the left with a family crest. Go through the gate to approach Arreton Manor **E**. Turn left to enter the Manor through the main entrance. Return through the small iron gate back to the footpath to the down.

Continue up the footpath along the edge of a field, with fence on right. At the top of the field, keep straight ahead up a narrow track that leads you up some steps to the foot of the open down.

8 There is no clear path at this point. The right-of-way you follow leads half-left diagonally up to the down to meet Downend

Road at the top. The best plan is to bear left for a few paces, keeping the thick hedges on your left. When the bushes turn further to the left, make your way up the down, aiming for the top left-hand corner. You will see a wooden stile on the corner just before you come to the hedge in front of Downend Road. Cross the stile, go straight over the road and take the narrow lane straight ahead. Follow this for about ½ mile (800 metres) and, when you see a lane leading right, turn left and cross the stile opposite. Ascend diagonally right, passing between the large trees to the electricity pole and stile beyond. Cross the stile and follow a pretty path through woods until you come to a lane.

9 You will see a house on the left, Rose Cottage. Look carefully, on your right, opposite the house for a wooden stile marked with a yellow arrow. Turn right over the stile. The route back to St George's Lane is marked with yellow arrows (more or less pointing in the right direction) but needs some careful navigation! From the stile bear half-left up the field to the corner of a hedge marked with a yellow arrow. Turn left (hedge on

left) down to metal gate. Cross two stiles, then turn right. Walk up the field to a stile a little to your left, just to the right of a strip of woodland. Cross the stile and keep straight on up the field, hedge on left. Go through the iron gate on your left at the top of the field and bear right (as yellow arrow indicates), hedge on your right, down the field. Cross the stile and bear half-left down the field to reach stile in the hedge at bottom.

10 Cross the stile and walk down the steps to cross a wooden footbridge. Bear left round the edge of the field (hedge on your left) towards a small building. Turn left to walk to the right of some ruined buildings.

11 Just past the buildings, do not go straight on but turn right down another track. After about 50 yards (45 metres), turn left to cross the line of the hedge, then bear right to a stile leading to the fringes of a wood. Follow the pretty woodland path to a stile leading to the golf course.

12 There is no clear path at this point. The right-of-way runs half-right, diagonally up the course. From the stile, walk towards a roof you will see on the skyline, to the right of a line of trees, to pick up

a hedge on your right. Ahead you will see a yellow arrow on one of the trees. This should point straight ahead but may have been tampered with. Continue ahead passing to right of the tree, through a metal gate along a grassy path with ancient trees, then Garrett's Farm on your right.

13 Just past the house, turn left over the stile. Your right-of-way here crosses the golf course to meet St George's Lane. There is no clear path, but the distance is very short. With your back to the stile, look over the green and you will see the outline of a small wood. Walk over the green aiming for the middle of the wood. The club house is about 100 yards (90 metres) on your right. Head for a point about 50 yards (45 metres) to the left of a corrugated iron building. Look for a small post marked with two yellow arrows which marks a narrow path leading through the gorse. Follow the path to cross a stile, a gravel track and another stile, to rejoin St George's Lane. Retrace your steps down the lane, then cross over the main road and the river and turn left along the footpath for Watergate Road, just past the Barley Mow.

National Wireless Museum and an enchanting 'Museum of Childhood'.

The return route is quite different. It rambles along quiet lanes and paths through some of the little inland valleys and oak woods that make up the heart of the island. Here you will find bluebells, wood-sorrel and the red squirrel in one of the last southern outposts.

Queen Victoria loved the Isle of Wight, and Newport retains much of its old-world Victorian charm. You will still find streets of small bow-fronted shops and dignified villas standing in spacious grounds. The Church of St Thomas the Apostle was rebuilt in Victorian

▶ *The church of St George in Arreton village dates from the 11th century. The prominent tower is late 13th-century.*

Arreton Manor

The Manor of Arreton belonged to King Alfred the Great, who left it to his son, Etherward, in his will made between AD 872 and 885. The present house was rebuilt on the site of an older one between 1595 and 1612, but part of the 14th-century house remains incorporated in the east wing. This includes a small kitchen approached through a hidden entrance down a twisting flight of stone steps. The entrance porch is later, dated 1639. The Hall retains another splendid feature of the earlier house, the Great Hall screen, erected in AD 1396.

▲*The return route from Arreton passes through quiet lanes and valleys with farmhouses in this agricultural area.*

One of the other rooms you will see is the Long Room, which contains a copy of King Alfred's will and the original will of Barnaby Leigh (tenant of the Manor during the reign of Elizabeth I). Barnaby's little daughter was murdered by her brother John, and her ghost is said to play happily about the house and garden! The West Bedroom, 'The Oak Room', contains a beautifully carved Tudor four-poster bed and a secret hide-away approached through the side of the chimney.

The Manor's allegiance to King Charles I is recalled by a fine print of the King and some of his possessions. A 300-year-old candlestick burns in his memory.

The elegant brick façade of Arreton Manor. Spanning Elizabethan and Jacobean periods, it has been owned by eight monarchs.

ing of special architectural and historic merit, is built of golden stone in the typical 'E' shape of late Elizabethan houses. The rooms are small, richly panelled and appropriately furnished. This beautiful house is home to several collections of bygones. The Museum of Childhood contains a wonderful collection of toys and dolls from many periods, and in a barn you will find the famous Pomeroy Regency doll's house. There is also a fine collection of lace. The National Wireless Museum has a unique collection of vintage wireless receivers.

▼*Great East Standen Manor, set in the folds of St George's Down, is surrounded by a profusion of flowers in spring.*

▲*This attractive sunken lane climbs to the top of St George's Down, with views of the Medina valley on the right.*

times. It contains a beautiful monument to Charles I's second daughter, Elizabeth, who died aged 15 during her imprisonment in Carisbrooke Castle.

The Roman Villa is small and compact, and it is possible for you to imagine just what life was like for the inhabitants. The villa faced south towards the downs, with a central suite of reception rooms approached across a verandah. This gave access to flanking wings, one housing a bath suite — each room survives — and the other the private family rooms with a separate bathing area.

OVER THE VALLEY

The view ◉ from this high point on St George's Down is superb. Across the Arreton Valley runs the curving sweep of the seaward-facing downs, with the stark white outline of Culver Cliff to the right. What appear to be inland rivers and lakes are acres of glasshouses where the early flowers and vegetables for which the island is well known are raised. The country craft village is the island's oldest established working craft centre. The church of St George in Arreton village was probably built in the 11th century, but retains features from an earlier Saxon church including a beautiful Saxon doorway and window.

Arreton Manor, listed as a build-

Exploring the varied scenery of a corner of the Isle of Wight

This walk of contrasts begins in an historic town, follows a causeway over marshland into farms and oak woods, then returns via a clifftop coastal path and chalk downland. On the way, you pass old buildings, modern holiday bungalows and military installations.

HISTORIC TOWN

Today, Brading **Ⓐ** seems little more than a village, but it was once known as 'Ye Kynge's Towne of Brading' and was a bustling, busy port on the River Yar. It has only been since 1880, when the Yar was dammed at its estuary in Bembridge, that Brading took on its

IAN PERT. INSET: ALAN WILLIAMS/NHPA

▲ *Splendid views of the massive chalk headland of Culver Cliff can be enjoyed from the coastal path above Whitecliff Bay. The rare marsh warbler (inset) can sometimes be seen on migration.*

FACT FILE

- ✳ Brading, 2 miles (3.2km) north-east of Sandown

- 🆗 Outdoor Leisure Map 29 , grid reference SZ 606873

miles 0	1	2	3	4	5	6	7	8	9	10 miles
kms 0	1 2 3 4 5 6 7 8 9 10	11 12 13 14 15 kms								

- 🕐 4 hours

- ▭ Suitable as family walk. Strong shoes recommended as chalk can be slippery when wet.

- 🅿 Car park by church in Brading

- 🚆 Trains to Brading from Ryde and Sandown. Frequent buses

- 🏛 Culver Haven, Culver Cliff; several pubs in Brading

- 🍴 Shops and restaurants in Brading

- 🚾 At the start

- 🏚 **I** Old Rectory and Wax Museum open daily, 10am–10pm May–Sept, 10am–5pm Oct–Apr. Lilliput Museum open mid-Mar to mid-Jan, 10am–5pm. Bembridge Windmill open Sun–Fri April–Oct, 10am–5pm; also Sat July–Aug

current quiet aspect, sheltering beneath tree-covered downs to the west and looking out over the marshland to the east.

It is a town steeped in history. Just to the south are the remains of a substantial Roman villa, famed for its mosaics. There was a Saxon settlement here, and Brading was already a busy port in AD704, when Bishop Wilfrid landed here to bring Christianity to the island. He built a church on the site of a pagan temple, on a ridge at the north of the town.

Today, the site is occupied by the 12th-century Church of St Mary, the largest medieval church on the island. It is distinguished by its porch-tower, which stands on arches so that a processional way could be made around the church without leaving consecrated ground, and, inside, by the monuments in the Oglander Chapel, dedicated to the family who lived in Nunwell House, just west of the town, until recently.

IAN PERT

Close by is the timber-framed Old Rectory Mansion, the oldest house on the island. A well-preserved building with a thatched roof and galleried courtyard, it now houses a collection of waxworks, which sheds an interesting light on Brading's history.

Across the High Street is the delightful Lilliput Antique Doll and Toy Museum, which has one of Britain's finest collections. You leave the town by an old lane which gives

◄ *Over 600 dolls, including one dated c.1790 and another owned by Queen Victoria, are found in this museum.*

on to a causeway across the Brading Marshes ❸, created by the damming of the Yar. Several varieties of duck cruise the shallow streams, while the thick sedge provides a nesting place for reed bunting and several types of warbler.

18TH-CENTURY WINDMILL

On the other side of the marshes, the route follows the Bembridge Trail through farmland, next to the airport, to Bembridge Windmill ❹. Four storeys high and built of local stone, the mill ground flour and meal, and later bran and cattle feed, for more than 200 years.

THE WALK

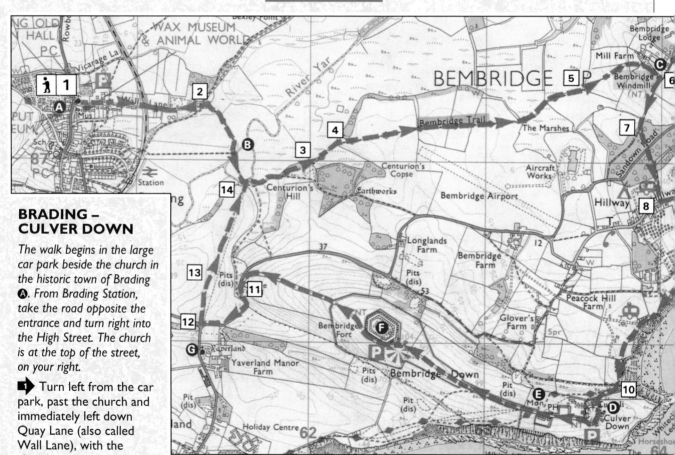

BRADING – CULVER DOWN

The walk begins in the large car park beside the church in the historic town of Brading ❹. From Brading Station, take the road opposite the entrance and turn right into the High Street. The church is at the top of the street, on your right.

▶ Turn left from the car park, past the church and immediately left down Quay Lane (also called Wall Lane), with the churchyard on your left and the Old Rectory Mansion on your right. Keep straight on past the last houses and down a lane with high hedges. Cross the railway. Ahead are the marshes around the River Yar ❸ Continue ahead to an iron gate.

▶ Go through the gate

and follow the footpath sign for Centurion's Copse and Bembridge. You are now on the Bembridge Trail, which runs along a causeway over the marshes. Cross the wooden bridge over a stream, climb the stile ahead, cross another

bridge and keep to the main path as it bears left through thickets of bracken and shrubs. When you come to a signpost, continue to follow the Bembridge Trail.

▶ A few paces further on, you come to a crosspath. Bear left and

keep on to climb a stile. The path now leads up the side of a field, with trees on your left, for about 150 yards (135m) until you are at the top of the rise.

▶ Here the path turns rather unexpectedly right. It is a sharper turn than the map would suggest. Look

IAN PERT

◄There has been a house on the site of the Wax Museum since at least 1228, though the current building is early Tudor. Just beyond is the 12th-century St Mary's Church, which contains many fine tombs. Bembridge Windmill (right), built around 1700, was in use until 1913.

▼*The Bembridge Trail runs along a causeway over the marshes and then continues through farmland.*

IAN PERT

across the middle of the island. Several species of gull are among the seabirds which nest on these cliffs, and peregrine falcons have been seen hunting here.

There are wonderful views to be had from the beacon on top of the Down, west over Sandown Bay and the English Channel and east over Bembridge Harbour and the Solent to the mainland. The guns here are the remains of a battery established in 1902 to guard the approaches to

It ceased production at the outbreak of World War I, but still retains much of its original 18th-century machinery. The National Trust now owns the mill and opens it to the public in the summer. Nearby, there is a wooden bench seat encircling a tree — just right for a rest and a snack.

The walk goes through Steyne Wood, an old oak woodland carpeted with ferns and flowers, and past Bembridge public school to the clifftop above Whitecliff Bay. The view ahead is dominated by the sheer white cliffs of Culver Down **Ⓓ**, the most easterly point of the great chalk ridge which serpentines

ISLE OF WIGHT TOURIST OFFICE

for a square tower on the horizon ahead of you. You pass a large tree on your left marked with yellow arrow footpath signs. The route leads over stiles and fields, and is clearly signposted 'Bembridge Trail'. On your right is Bembridge Airport.

5▶ The path bears left here as it begins to climb the down. Cross the stile and walk up the hill towards a farmhouse. Just before the farm, bear half right on the Bembridge Trail to come to Bembridge Windmill **Ⓒ**.

6▶ Just past the windmill, turn right, following the bridleway sign for Steyne Wood. This lovely path

drops steeply down into the old oak wood.

7▶ A few paces into the wood, fork left along a path which quickly brings you to the B3395 Sandown Road. Cross straight over and follow the footpath immediately ahead through the trees to a minor road.

8▶ Turn left and look for a footpath sign on your right-hand side. Turn right and follow the path until you come to a lane.

9▶ Bear left for a few yards and you will see the footpath continuing right towards the cliff. At the clifftop, turn right along the coastal path and follow it as it curves around Whitecliff Bay towards the massive

chalk headland of Culver Cliff. You pass a caravan site on your right-hand side, and begin to climb past holiday bungalows.

10▶ Cross the stile onto the open hillside and climb to the top of Culver Down **Ⓓ**. Bear left to meet a little road that encircles the summit of the headland. Follow the road round to the left, past the gun emplacements. There is a beacon and a splendid viewpoint on your right. Follow the road over Bembridge Down, past the Monument **Ⓔ** and Bembridge Fort **Ⓕ** to a cattle grid leading to the B3395 Sandown Road.

11▶ Turn left and follow the road until you come to the

turning for Yaverland on your left. The Jacobean manor and church **Ⓖ** are clearly visible on your left.

12▶ Turn right on the footpath opposite the Yaverland turning. Cross over the stile on the other side of the field.

13▶ There is no clear path at this point. From the stile, walk very slightly right, aiming just to the right of a belt of woodland you will see ahead. Look for a stile leading to a path through the trees beside the Bembridge Trail.

14▶ Cross the stile and follow the path ahead to rejoin the Bembridge Trail. Turn left and retrace your steps back to Brading.

▲*Brading Marshes, in the middle distance, provide good nesting habitat for ducks, waders and various warblers.*

the Spithead. The two emplacements of nine 2-inch (5mm) breach-loading guns were in action during both World Wars and were used for training purposes until 1956.

CRESTING THE DOWN

The walk takes a road along the crest of Bembridge Down, past a monument ❸ erected in 1849 to the first Earl of Yarborough, founder of the Royal Yacht Squadron. This road and its verges are owned by the National Trust. To encourage the growth of downland flowers, the Trust runs a flock of sheep on the land to close-crop the turf.

The Trust also owns the land around Bembridge Fort ❺, which was built between 1862 and 1867 as part of Lord Palmerston's sea defences. During World War I, its heavy artillery was used as a coastal defence and, in World War II, it was an anti-aircraft post and the

The Queen of Chantilly

The life of the beautiful local girl, Sophie Dawes, is a remarkable rags-to-riches story. She was born in 1792, the illegitimate daughter of a smuggler. After a childhood spent in the workhouse at Newport, she scratched a living picking winkles on Bembridge beach, before leaving the island at the age of 15.

Within 30 years, she was one of the richest women in France, moving in the highest society and elevated to the rank of Baroness. The French called her the Queen of Chantilly.

Sophie left the island to work as a chambermaid in the George Hotel in Portsmouth, but soon went on to London. There, in a house of ill repute, she met the Duc de Bourbon, who was captivated by her. Wisely, Sophie used the money he gave her to take lessons in music, French and the Classics. When the Duc returned to Paris in 1814, she was well prepared to take her place in society as his mistress.

Immensely rich, she divided her time between her chateau at Chantilly and the Palais de Bourbon in Paris. She persuaded the heir to the French throne, the Duc d'Orléans, to receive her at court; in return, she promised that Orléans' son would inherit the de Bourbon estates. At first, de Bourbon agreed but later it was rumoured that he intended to change his will. Soon afterwards, he was murdered.

Sophie Dawes' remarkable beauty and fulsome charms are revealed in this model in Brading's Wax Museum.

Sophie came under suspicion, and quickly returned to England, where she bought the Bure Homage estate near Christchurch and a house in London. She died in London in 1840.

The cottage where Sophie was born can be seen beside the green in St Helens, close to Bembridge, and her wax image is displayed in Brading's Wax Museum.

▼*From the road, you can get a fine view of Yaverland Manor, a substantial Jacobean house built in 1620.*

headquarters of the local Home Guard. It is now leased to a manufacturing company. Geese are kept in the moat to warn of anyone's approach, as they did on the Capitol in Ancient Rome.

JACOBEAN MANOR

After descending from the Down onto a road, there are fine views to your right of Yaverland Manor, a Jacobean house built by the Richards family in 1620, and the restored Norman church attached to it ❻. The Manor is private, and best seen from the road. From here, a short walk across the flanks of a chalk hill takes you back to the beginning of the causeway across the marshes, and thence to Brading itself.

ALL PHOTOS: IAN PERT

rendition of Daniel in the lions' den. Inside, there is some good work from the 13th and 14th centuries and some box pews.

The route heads south on a lovely path beside a stream, the Caul Bourne, and passes through little copses of old oaks, where flowers abound. There are lovely downland views as the path rises over the track

A family walk to a lovely village and a fascinating mill

The Isle of Wight is like a garden, with richly varied landscapes enclosed within a small area. This walk, which follows a stream through the heart of the western part of the island, explores a gentle, watery area of low, rolling hills and mill streams decorated with wild flowers. It visits one of the island's prettiest villages and a mill that now has something for the whole family.

You begin in Shalfleet, a cluster of

▲*Winkle Street in Calbourne runs between a row of old stone cottages and a clear chalk stream edged with yellow flag. The peacock (inset) is one of the birds to be seen at Calbourne Mill.*

old stone cottages, mostly thatched, around an old inn — paradoxically called the New Inn — on the main Newport to Yarmouth road. The village stands at the head of a picturesque inlet, with a quay nearly 1 mile (1.6km) to the north that gives splendid views of the Solent.

MASSIVE TOWER

Shalfleet is dominated by its church **A**, which was mentioned in the *Domesday Book*. The massive tower dates from the 11th century. It was built with walls 5 feet (1.5m) thick as a place of refuge from French raiders; originally, there was no entry to it at ground level. The 12th-century south doorway is surmounted by a tympanum, on which there is a crude but appealing

◀*This charming carving in the Norman doorway of Shalfleet's church is thought to represent Daniel in the lions' den.*

FACT FILE

⁂ Shalfleet, 5½ miles (8.8km) west of Newport, on the A3054

⊡ Pathfinder 1335 (SZ 28/38 & part of SZ 48) or Outdoor Leisure Map 29, grid reference SZ 414892

miles 0	1	2	3	4	5	6	7	8	9	10 miles
kms 0	1 2 3	4 5	6 7	8 9 10	11	12 13	14 15	kms		

◑ Allow at least 3½ hours

▬ Easy walking on lanes and footpaths over gently undulating country. Can be muddy in parts; strong shoes or boots are recommended

P Car park down the lane beside The New Inn

T The Lymington to Yarmouth ferry runs approximately hourly, Tel. (01705) 827744 for details. A bus service operates from Yarmouth to Shalfleet

▤ The New Inn at Shalfleet

▯ Calbourne Mill has a tea-room

⌹ Calbourne Mill is open from Easter to October, Tel. (01983) 531227. Admission charge

bed of a disused old railway.

Across the valley stands New bridge Mill **B**. This was reopened in 1973 after many years' disuse, and produces a high-quality stone-ground flour. Bakers use this to make wheat wafers, a special island

▶ *Newbridge Mill, now used as a house, stands near the Caul Bourne.*

IAN PERT

THE WALK

SHALFLEET – CALBOURNE

The walk starts from The New Inn at Shalfleet.

1 Cross the main road and go down Church Lane past the church **A**. When the lane curves right, go left down a grassy path signposted to Newbridge. At the field, keep straight on to cross a plank bridge. Climb a stile and follow the stream on your left until you see a fence directly ahead.

2 The path leaves the side of the stream and bears half-right up the field to a public footpath sign (this may be obscured by foliage in summer). Cross the stile by the sign and go ahead over the track of the disused railway, past a farm and down a lane.

3 Where the lane bears left downhill, opposite Newbridge Mill **B**, go straight on over a stile. Continue ahead over fields and stiles to a minor road.

4 Turn right, then almost immediately left down Clay Lane to a footpath sign showing three directions. (Take note of this junction, you will return here later). Go left, signposted 'Newbridge/Calbourne Road'. Follow the path round to the left, then down into a wood. Continue over a plank bridge and uphill to a crosspath. (The path is very narrow at this point but if you look left you will see the crosspath meeting a bend in a road.)

5 Turn right and continue along the narrow path. Cross a plank bridge and climb a stile. The path bears a little left and continues beside the Caul Bourne for a few paces, then divides.

6 Ignore the more obvious route (left over the stream), and continue straight ahead on an ill-defined path. Go ahead over two stiles, with a plank bridge between, to a road. Go straight over and down the bridleway, signposted to Westover. Pass a farmhouse on your right and continue to a crossing track in front of some farm buildings.

7 Turn left. The track enters a wood. As it bears right, look for a waymarked stile on your left. Cross and follow a narrow track through a copse and across a plank bridge to another waymarked stile.

8 Follow the waymark across a meadow, aiming just to the left of some trees. Continue straight ahead across another meadow, downhill and over the Caul Bourne by means of a plank bridge.

9 Turn immediately right on the path by the stream. This becomes Winkle Street **C**. At the top of the street, bear left to cross the road and climb the steps to Calbourne's church. Continue up the village and turn left down School Lane. Keep straight on down a narrow, grassy path to a stile into a field. Continue straight ahead over fields and stiles to some steps leading down to a road. Turn left and follow it to Calbourne Mill **D** on your right.

10 After visiting the mill, follow the footpath signposted 'Newbridge' to a stile. Go over the stile and across the field, bearing a little right, towards the Caul Bourne. Follow the stream across a tributary stream and turn right to retrace your earlier steps to the junction of paths you noted in Stage 4. Follow the bridleway signposted Ningwood and Chessel Road and follow it to a lane. Turn right and follow the lane to a T-junction. Go straight ahead along the bridleway signposted to Shalfleet. Keep straight on over the old railway to a lane. Turn right and follow the lane as it bends left, right and left again.

11 About 100 yards (90m) before a T-junction with a main road, turn right down a lane marked 'No Through Road'. Follow this round Shalfleet's church back to the start.

shortbread and Calbourne crunchies, a local delicacy available in shops throughout Wight.

The route goes through Newbridge and down Clay Lane, a high-hedged lane edged with cow parsley and cuckoo pint, then climbs gently through woods and over streams to Westover Farm. From the farm, there are spreading views north to the creeks and estuaries on the Solent, and south towards the chalk downs that form the backbone of the island.

HONEY-COLOURED STONE

You drop down again to the Caul Bourne and a path that becomes Winkle Street ● as it leads into the village of Calbourne. The street comprises a picturesque row of tiled and thatched cottages in honey-coloured local stone opposite grassy lawns and a stream edged with flowers and ferns. To enter Winkle Street from the wood is a delightfully medieval experience.

The village boasts another church of ancient foundation, built on land

▼ *The present buildings of Calbourne Mill are 17th century, but there has been a mill here for over 900 years.*

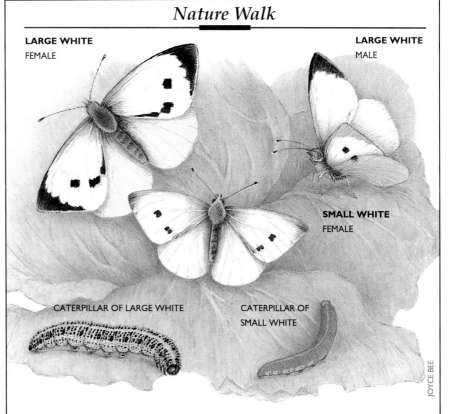

Nature Walk

LARGE WHITE
FEMALE

LARGE WHITE
MALE

SMALL WHITE
FEMALE

CATERPILLAR OF LARGE WHITE

CATERPILLAR OF SMALL WHITE

JOYCE BEE

CABBAGE WHITES Feeding on cabbages and Brussels sprouts, these caterpillars are the only British butterfly larvae to damage crops. The adult large white is noticeably larger than the small white, which has a 2"/5cm wingspan. The dark markings on the large white are usually blacker than those of its relative.

IAN PERT

granted by King Egbert in AD826. Inside, there is a perfectly preserved brass dating from 1579. It commemorates William Muntacute, a son of the Earl of Salisbury, who was accidentally killed while jousting with his father. The heartbroken earl ordered a commemorative brass to be placed in the church of every parish where he held lands.

WORKING MILL

The way out of the village, past an old iron pump beneath a tiled roof, is down a lane that, like Winkle Street, peters out into a path. This leads to Calbourne Mill ❶, superbly set in a wooded valley. A fine example of a working 17th-century mill, its great overshot wheel turns two pairs of millstones. The important role that mills played in the lives of our ancestors (see box) is displayed in fascinating detail, and visitors are free to wander around the grounds.

Peafowl and a variety of ducks and other waterbirds roam freely

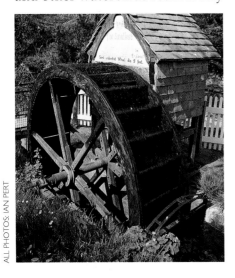

ALL PHOTOS: IAN PERT

▲ *This semi-undershot mill wheel at Calbourne Mill is said to be the smallest working example in England.*

and can be hand fed, while a stroll along the stream reveals other fascinating features, including a steam-engine built originally for the Liverpool Garden Festival, and a working millwheel just 9 feet (2.7m) in diameter.

The return to Shalfleet retraces part of the outward route, then goes off along green bridleways and quiet lanes to explore more of the pleasant pastoral landscape of this corner of the garden-island.

Calbourne Mill

The interior of Calbourne Mill is filled with fascinating old equipment.

Calbourne has had a watermill since at least the *Domesday Book* in 1086. Today's mill came into the possession of the present family in 1878, and they decided to preserve the 17th-century buildings as a working example of agricultural life in days gone by.

The great water wheel measures 20 feet (6m) in diameter. Its buckets scoop through a sluice from a feed tank. Every hour, 126,000 gallons (573kl) of water flow over the wheel; this means that each pound (2.2kg) of meal requires 225 gallons (1kl) of water.

During the 19th century, Calbourne Mill survived because its owners were enterprising enough to install roller plant driven by a portable steam engine (a similar working engine can be seen in the grounds). This was replaced in 1920 by a suction gas engine of about 30 horsepower, which was used until 1955 and is still in place today.

Stoneground flour goes off quickly, so the mill had its own bakehouse and malthouse. The old ovens can be seen, together with a fascinating collection of farm and domestic implements that date from the last 100 years. These range from a 1920 Ruston diesel engine — once used to power a laundry in Yarmouth by day and to operate a dynamo to provide electricity for most of the village by night — to small, everyday items like bean dibbers and a marvellous device that held a horse's mouth open while he was dosed with medicine.

A visit to 'Grandma's Kitchen' is rewarded by nostalgic glimpses into homes of the past 50 to 100 years, with a background of world events provided by items from the two World Wars. There is a great deal to see at Calbourne Mill, so allow plenty of time to enjoy it all.

The engine museum has examples of the machines that took over from water power.